DESIGNER DOGS

PORTRAITS AND PROFILES OF POPULAR NEW CROSSBREEDS

Words

Caroline Coile

Pictures

Anna Kuperberg

GOLD ST.
PRESS

GOLD ST. PRESS

Published by Gold Street Press,
a division of Weldon Owen Inc.
814 Montgomery Street
San Francisco, CA 94133
www.goldstreetpress.com

WELDON OWEN GROUP

Chief Executive Officer John Owen
Chief Financial Officer Simon Fraser

WELDON OWEN INC.

President, Chief Executive Officer Terry Newell
Vice President, International Sales Stuart Laurence
Vice President, Sales & Marketing Amy Kaneko
Vice President, Publisher Roger Shaw
Vice President, Creative Director Gaye Allen
Art Director, Designer Marisa Kwek
Assistant Designer Stephanie Tang
Photo Coordinator Meghan Hildebrand
Executive Editor Mariah Bear
Managing Editor Peter Cieply
Assistant Editor Lucie Parker
Production Director Chris Hemesath
Production Manager Michelle Duggan
Color Manager Teri Bell
Prop Stylist Deborah Dapolito

A WELDON OWEN PRODUCTION
© 2007 Weldon Owen Inc.

Library of Congress Control Number: 2007828031

ISBN-13: 978-1-934533-00-0
ISBN-10: 1-934533-00-9

10 9 8 7 6 5 4 3 2 1

Printed by SNP Leefung in China.

Contents

Canine Design

Ever since the first dog decided to buddy up with a human 15,000 years ago, the two species have been cultivating a friendship of legendary proportions, one based on both survival and companionship. These days, you see dogs and their people hobnobbing harmoniously everywhere you go. Whether petite and plush or big and burly, robust and rugged or svelte and sophisticated, there's a perfect pet for every dog lover out there. And now, the choice of canine companions is ever-expanding, thanks to new attention paid to "designer dogs," more commonly referred to as crossbreeds, or hybrids.

It's no mystery as to why these dogs are so popular today. In our jet-set world, everything is made to order. Custom cars, custom clothes, custom homes—it was only a matter of time before we got around to custom canines. Actually, the concept is nothing new. Long before the ancient Romans were buying designer togas, purpose-bred dogs were all the rage. Our ancestors had fast dogs to run down game, massive dogs to fight enemies, and tiny dogs to adorn laps. Over the ensuing centuries, breeders crossed a little of this to a little of that, let it settle, and started over again, until they'd created canine specialists to fill all niches—hunting, herding, guarding, toting, and just keeping company. Today, as many as 750 breeds exist in the world, and the American Kennel Club (AKC) recognizes about 150 of them. But that still doesn't seem to be enough; after all, it's human nature to seek the unique.

Late in the nineteenth century, dogs went from being regarded as families of animals that could be bred to other families when the need arose, to being treated as purebreds, complete with pedigrees, that must be bred only among themselves. Owning a pedigreed dog was a sure sign of affluence and taste, and in the first half of the twentieth century, no socialite worth her salt would be seen with a crossbreed at the end of her leash. But as purebred begat purebred, the supply for these dogs began to exceed the society set's demand for them, and little by little, fancy dogs became available to regular folk.

Jump to the twentieth century's end, when just about anybody could buy a purebred by perusing the listings in the paper or visiting a pet store. Given this democratization, purebreds were no longer seen as status symbols, and the elite lost interest.

A new dog for a new era

These days, the "beautiful people" are frequently seen sporting a different sort of dog: crossbreeds, often rescued from shelters. Some of these mixes are so adorable that people have begun wanting their own dogs just like them, and breeders have found a new market among those who want so-called designer dogs—breeds not found in the AKC registry.

Of course, crossing breeds is hardly a modern development: that's how most pedigreed breeds got their start. Many purebreds were once crosses, and most are mixes of several breeds. The difference between those and today's hybrids, though, is that those dogs were then bred among themselves and selected for desired characteristics generation after generation, forming their own distinctive breed. Designer dogs are (almost) always the first-generation cross of purebreds.

Today's designer dogs may be trendsetters, but they're still following in others' paw prints. Way back in the 1960s, Cockapoos (first-generation crosses of Cocker Spaniels and Poodles) gained an ardent following, and Pekeapoos

(Pekingese-Poodle crosses) were yapping at their heels. Back then, though, they weren't called designer dogs. They were viewed as purebred wannabes, not as posh pooches.

The Australian Labradoodle changed all that. First bred in 1988 with the aim of creating a hypoallergenic guide dog for the blind, this breed fell short of its original mission (it wasn't sufficiently sneeze-proof), but a remarkable thing happened. Its catchy name, broadcast to attract parents for the potential guide dogs, attracted scores of people who wanted one as a pet. Demand soared to the point that they soon commanded far higher prices than their purebred parents. The sensation then spread, resulting in the creation of an American version. Hot on the Labradoodle's heels was the Goldendoodle, but diminutive designer dogs, aided by celebrity owners, soon took over as the darlings of the hybrid world.

Science steps in

Another factor that sparked the designer-dog revolution was media reports about hereditary health problems in purebreds. To understand this, you need to know a bit about genetics, as well as a bit about how purebreds were classified and mated.

When kennel clubs began registering purebreds, they allowed any dog of that general family type to be registered as the breed. At some point, registrations closed, leaving a fixed number of potential canine fathers and mothers (called sires and dams). What wasn't known at that time was that all of us, dog or human, carry from five to seven recessive genes that, if we carried two copies of any one of them, would result in some type of hereditary disease. Because humans are a bunch of mixed breeds, we don't often end up with a mate who

carries the same bad recessive gene as we do, so it's unusual to produce an affected child. In at least purebred dogs, it's different. Because those early canine sires and dams carried some random bad recessives, and because all present-day purebred dogs descend from them, there's a fair chance that dogs carrying that same recessive gene might mate, creating a puppy with the disorder caused by that recessive gene.

The solution? Widen the breeding options, deepen the gene pools to create crossbreeds that don't share the same bad recessives. That's one argument for breeding dogs by design. The trouble is that idea works only within limits. Cross two breeds that share the same disorders and it doesn't work at all. Cross two hybrids again after the first initial cross, and you're right back where you started—maybe even worse off: those hybrids will stand a good chance of carrying recessive genes and producing pups with two of the recessives and thus a disorder. Any good breeder will study the genetics and health problems of each parent breed, screen for these problems, and avoid breeding parents that share the disorder. A designer dog should never be just a random mating "to see what happens." Instead, the best mixes blend breeds that can reasonably be expected to produce desirable physical and behavioral traits.

The advantage of purebred dogs is their predictability. To a degree, you can pretty much know how big they'll get, how they'll look, and even how they'll act. Generations of selection have produced dogs that live to retrieve, hunt, dig, run, herd, pull, fight, or snuggle. Fortunately, the first-generation cross of purebreds is equally predictable: crossbreed dogs bred from two good purebred representatives should look and act like other crossbreed dogs from the same parent breeds.

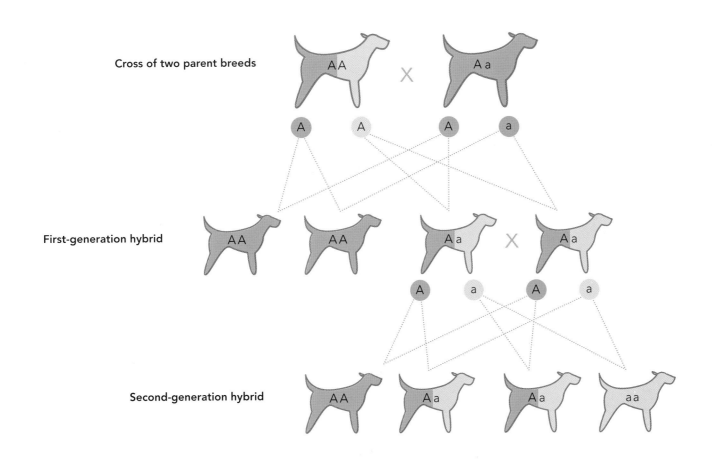

Cross of two parent breeds

First-generation hybrid

Second-generation hybrid

Heredity and health

A   dominant gene

a   recessive gene

 AA

 Aa

aa

To understand why only a first-generation cross is effective in avoiding some hereditary problems, you have to play science geek. In genetic lingo, a dominant gene is designated by an uppercase letter, and a recessive one by a lowercase letter. It takes two recessive genes, one inherited from each parent, for a dog to exhibit a recessively inherited disorder. (There are also dominantly inherited disorders, where only the presence of one gene is needed for the disease to occur, but they're just as likely in purebreds as in mixes.) Assume a Pug has one dominant and one recessive gene, A and a (Aa).

She is bred to a Beagle who has two A genes (AA). On average, half of their puppies will be AA, and half will be Aa, but none will be affected with the recessive disorder. If her puppies are bred to one another, however, there's a chance an Aa sire will mate with an Aa dam, and they may produce puppies that are AA, Aa, and aa. The aa puppies will be affected with the disorder. That's why anything beyond first-generation crosses are no healthier than their parent breeds. In fact, they may be less so, because they'll contend with the combined genetic baggage of both parent breeds.

A Perfect Pet

Selecting the right designer dog entails more than simply finding one that's cute. It's like choosing an outfit. Sure, you might fall in love with one on a runway model, but that doesn't mean it's going to be a practical fit for you or your lifestyle. The same is true for dogs. Those bred to be hunters tend to follow their noses, wander away, and maybe show back up with a gift of a dead rat, to the chagrin of some people. Those bred to be retrievers may spend all day and night insisting on playing with slobbery tennis balls, which doesn't thrill others.

To figure out which crossbreed is right for you, it's best to study up on today's popular hybrids, noting their activity levels, temperaments, grooming requirements, barking tendencies, and trainability ratings. Sneaking a peek at the qualities and dispositions of their purebred parents will also help you understand where a hybrid's character traits come from, and if those traits will be compatible with your way of living.

The right dog for you

Fads and fashions come and go, but dogs will outlive trends by years. When choosing a pet, remember that a dog is a long-term commitment, a friend who will stick by you, thick and thin, and a real member of your family—a passion, not a fashion. Keep in mind that if it's a unique dog you're looking for, consider the true one-of-a-kind design canine: a shelter mutt in need of a special place in somebody's home and heart.

But if you decide you do want a designer dog, you'll need to study up a bit. If finding the ideal designer dog were easy, everyone would have one, right? You wouldn't expect to find a fine designer gown at a roadside stand or at the mall. Don't expect to find a great designer dog in those places, either.

One challenge in finding a designer dog, as opposed to a purebred, is that few hybrids have breed clubs devoted to them. Such clubs often help guide you to well-regarded and ethical breeders. But since you'll be on your own shopping for a designer dog, remember this: the best breeders make sure their puppies go to homes where they'll be loved and cared for.

The right breeder

A reputable breeder should quiz you about your experience with dogs, your facilities, and your family. They will discuss expenses, exercise, training, grooming, health care, and safety issues with you. They'll require that you neuter or spay your dog. They may ask you to wait several months for a litter, and during this "cooling-off period" they can make sure you're not just impulse buying. They'll tell you everything bad about their crossbreeds as well as what's good—no hybrid is perfect for everyone, and upstanding breeders want you to know any disadvantages before you find out the hard way. If a breeder doesn't care where the puppies are going, there's a fair chance very little thought went into breeding and raising them.

The right things to ask

Keep these questions in mind when you begin to evaluate breeders and choose among puppies in a litter.

How many types of dogs are bred?
Breeders who always have puppies, or who have several different breeds, probably can't give each litter the attention it deserves, and may not know enough about each breed or cross to do a responsible job breeding it. Select breeders who concentrate on just one or two types of purebreds or hybrids.

Are references from a veterinarian or past buyers available?
This is especially important if you must buy from a source you can't visit in person, such as a breeder found on the Internet.

Can you visit the facilities?
If not, look elsewhere. If yes, look carefully. Dogs and their surroundings should be clean and well kept, and should have ample room to run and play. If the dogs live their entire lives in small cages or never get to interact with people, take it as a sign that this breeder doesn't have the welfare of dogs in mind.

Where are the puppies raised?
Ideally, you want your puppy to grow up in a breeder's home, not in a kennel or garage. If puppies are raised in small pens in which they must relieve themselves, they can be difficult to house-train because they've already formed bad habits. Look for puppies that are raised as part of the family, with lots of human interaction, outdoor play, and access to potty areas.

Can you meet the parents?
The sire may not live on the premises, but you should be able to meet the dam. She should be well groomed and have the sort of personality you'd like your puppy to have.

Have the parents been screened for hereditary health issues?
Purebred parents should have the health clearances necessary for their respective breeds. Here's where you have to know your crossbreeds and what health problems they're susceptible to: just because they're hybrids doesn't mean they're immune from common disorders. Good breeders screen their breeding stock for as many hereditary problems as possible, and ask for health reports from owners of the puppies they have produced. By collecting as much information on every dog in the line, they

become aware of health problems and work to eradicate them. (See pages 156–157 for more specific health information.)

When can you get your puppy?
The best time to bring a new puppy home is between seven and twelve weeks of age. Beware the breeder who will part with a puppy that's younger than seven, or preferably eight, weeks of age. Before seven weeks, removing a puppy from its dam and littermates deprives it of learning essential canine social skills. In addition, very small puppies are susceptible to medical conditions brought on by stress or hunger that can be life-threatening, so unless you're home a lot or are experienced with dogs, it may not be a good idea to take one so young. On the other hand, after twelve weeks, puppies become more fearful of new situations (if the breeder has taken measures to expose an older puppy to new experiences and people, then the puppy should be able to make the transition just fine).

What about the puppies?
They should be friendly toward you; avoid any that are shy or that are overly independent. Their eyes, ears, and noses should be free of discharge, and they should show no signs of diarrhea. Make any sale contingent upon a veterinary examination within forty-eight hours. Your veterinarian is in the best position to evaluate the puppy's health. The breeder should supply all vaccinations and worming records.

Is there a pedigree?
Your designer dog is not a pedigreed dog, but both her parents should have a pedigree. A pedigree shows that your dog's parents, while of different breeds, were themselves purebred. Some of her distant ancestors might have been show champions—your dog may come from royalty!

Meet the Parents

There are a whopping 750 or so breeds of dogs thought to exist throughout the world, and although the AKC only registers 155 breeds, some international registries recognize more than 400 of them. Many of these breeds have become known for the qualities that they bring to a match, and so are favored parents of designer dogs. But with new matches being conjured up daily, you need a program just to keep up. You can make a good guess about personality, however, by looking at what role a breed was created to perform, and you can get a hint about that by studying up on how breeds are classified.

Sporting dogs are all about birds. Pointers and setters are revved-up, nonstop, four-legged bird locators. They tend to range far afield, and have lots of energy. Retrievers have a compulsion to fetch anything you try to throw away. They're usually more obedient, but get used to slimy tennis balls being a staple around your home. Spaniels both locate and retrieve, so they're kind of in between the other two.

Hounds are all about the hunt, but they're into fur, not feathers. Scent hounds sniff out a scent and they're drawn to it as if by a magnet. Sight hounds catch sight of fleeing fur and they'll run it down like a cheetah on a gazelle. Try calling a scent hound or sight hound off the hunt—they won't hear you. Try telling them what to do, and they'll pretend they don't hear at all.

Working dogs are the menial force of the dog world. They include bodyguards, livestock guards, and junkyard dogs, all tough guys who aren't afraid of a little action. But they have to take orders, and they're not bad at it. Other members of the canine working class include the beasts of burden, the draft dogs, and the sled dogs, who tend to be tireless.

Terriers are the tough guys of dogdom. They don't mind taking on equally tough characters, and they don't back down. They also don't back down when you tell them to do something. They're energetic, inquisitive, mischievous, stubborn—and nonstop fun.

Toy dogs are doll-sized versions of full-scale breeds. They may look like lapdogs, they may even play like lapdogs, but deep down, they're dogs, and they like to do the same things that their larger counterparts do.

Non-sporting dogs are the grab-bag dogs, some would even say the misfits—dogs without a proper group of their own to call home. Many of them were once gainfully employed, but are now jobless due to progress. Some were just bred to be companions in the first place.

Herding dogs are the round-'em-up dogs of the world, regular control freaks when it comes to sheep and cattle. The good part is that they don't mind being controlled in turn by people, and they're quick to follow orders.

If you cross dogs with similar traits, you can guess the offspring will share those traits, but if you go where no breeder has gone before and cross dogs with contrasting traits, it's anybody's guess. What's absolutely not possible to say is that the hybrids from them will only inherit the best of both breeds. Genes don't know good from bad, or what you want and don't want in a dog. A cross is just as likely to get the worst of both breeds. Besides, what one person considers desirable another might find deplorable—that's the reason for so many types of dogs, and why the quest for the right dog may never end.

Actress Audrey Hepburn

Fashion Designer Kate Spade

Poodle   There's a reason the names of so many crossbreeds end in "-poo" or "-oodle." It's the same reason the Poodle is one of dogdom's all-time sweethearts: they're smart looking and acting. Classic sporting dogs, Poodles were developed as duck-hunting retrievers and through the years have played the roles of military dog, guide dog, guard dog, circus performer, and status symbol, before reaching their zenith as companions. Lively and always eager to play or learn, Poodles excel at just about everything they do. They come in three sizes, Toy, Miniature, and Standard, and weigh between 4 and 65 pounds (2–30 kg). The Poodle palette comes in a wide variety of colors, including spotted (although the AKC does not consider spotted Poodles acceptable, unlike other international registries). Their low-shedding hair is said to be hypoallergenic, but that claim is often overstated, as it takes more than hair to trigger allergies. Although the list of "doodles" and "poos" is lengthy, the Labradoodle (featured on page 89), the Cockapoo (page 45), and the Schnoodle (page 131) are among the most popular.

Maltese   Talk about withstanding the test of time: the jaunty Maltese is among the most ancient of all breeds, specifically mentioned as early as 300 B.C. By the fourteenth century, representative cuties of this toy breed traveled to Europe to become the darlings of upper-crust ladies. Maltese can lay claim to being lapdogs longer than any other breed, but that doesn't mean all they do is hang out on laps. They like to run and play, and don't let those Bambi eyes fool you—these dogs are bold and feisty, with a mind of their own. Of course, they do the lap thing, too, and do it well. It doesn't hurt that they are one of the smallest breeds, weighing in at under 7 pounds (3 kg). Their hallmark is their luxurious cape of brilliant white hair that can trail on the ground. They come in an extensive choice of colors, as long as you like white. Maltese have been used to create several hybrids, most notably the Maltapoo (featured on page 123). Not far behind in the ranks, the Malshi (page 103), the Maltipom (page 107), and the Yorktese (page 141) continue to garner accolades as adorable up-and-comers.

Television Personality Kathie Lee Gifford

First Lady Jacqueline Kennedy Onassis, with children

Bichon Frise The comeback kid of the dog world, the Bichon Frise started life as a privileged pet of the upper class, remaining so from the fourteenth to the nineteenth century, when for some reason it plummeted from favor. It fell from court darling to common street dog, joining up with peddlers and organ grinders to entertain passersby for handouts. It wasn't until the 1930s that the dainty and exuberant Bichon Frise caught the attention of a few modern pet owners, with another fifty years passing before people realized what they'd been missing. Playful and perky, these white puffballs with the happy-go-lucky outlook endear themselves to everyone. They're as eager to cuddle as to play, and they're quick to learn. They typically weigh between 10 and 16 pounds (5–7 kg), and their poodle-like coat comes in white, possibly with cream shading. The Cavachon (featured on page 25) is their most popular hybrid offspring, but the Yochon (page 95), the Zuchon (page 101), and the Silkchon (page 139) are on their way to securing heartthrob status as well.

Pug Multum in Parvo (a lot in a little): that's the Pug's official motto, and it's a fitting one, because few other dogs can cram as much zest for life into a body as small as this ancient Chinese dog's. After conquering China with their impish antics and aristocratic airs, ambassadors of this toy breed made their way to Europe, where they became the prized pups of royalty. They filled in as court jesters whenever they could, including for King Edward VIII. Natural-born clowns and show-offs even today, their pranks are made even more whimsical by their dignified mugs and assortment of snorts and snuffles. Sure, they're stubborn, but nobody cares—they're too cute! Pugs have flat faces, with abundant wrinkles that add to their perpetually bemused expressions. While they're active and playful, they aren't known athletes, due to their short snouts. Their hair is short and coarse, and comes in fawn, silver, or black, always with a black muzzle. They weigh in at 14 to 18 pounds (6–8 kg), and are one of the parents of the ever-popular Puggle (featured on page 133), as well as the Frenchie Pug (page 81).

Comedian Jerry Lewis

President Lyndon B. Johnson

Shih Tzu Spunky but sweet, the Shih Tzu has been ruling from laps since ancient times. A particularly favored house pet of Chinese royalty during the Ming dynasty, the toy breed was almost wiped out when the British looted the Imperial Palace. They emerged slowly into the Western spotlight, with numbers so low that as recently as 1952 the AKC allowed the progeny of a Shih Tzu–Pekingese cross to register and then mate with purebred Shih Tzus, all in an effort to expand the breed's gene pool. Nowadays, these deluxe dogs are seen far and wide, noted for their striking coifs and regal manners. They have a high opinion of themselves, and are a bit headstrong. But they're also playful and upbeat, and extremely loving with their special people. They weigh in at 9 to 16 pounds (4–7 kg), fitting on most laps with ease. Their long and luxurious hair, which can mop the floor, comes in almost any color. Shih Tzus are not as popular a hybrid parent as some others, but the Zuchon (featured on page 101) and the Malshi (page 103) are endearing examples of this breed's genetic contributions.

Beagle If there were such a thing as an official best friend of dogdom, the Beagle would be it. Bred as pack hounds, they thrive on companionship, human or canine. They're pals to all, and super-affectionate with their special people—and pretty much everyone else. Maybe that's why they've remained a stalwart of the list of top-ten favorite breeds in America. But Beagles were bred to hunt, and they've got a nose for trouble and an eye for adventure. Known wanderers, it's no secret that they're hard to train. Luckily for them, their trademark soulful Beagle eyes get them out of most of the trouble they get themselves into. They come in two sizes: the cute 13 inch (33 cm), for dogs not exceeding that height at the shoulder, and the handsome 15 inch (38 cm), for dogs between 13 inches and 15 inches in height. Their bodies are often brown with white extremities and a black saddle, but they can come white with spots, and all sorts of colors. The Beagle is one parent of the famous Puggle (featured on page 133), and also contributes charms to the Bagle Hound (page 39) and the Labbe (page 51).

Prince Charles

Actor Errol Flynn

Labrador Retriever Labs have been America's favorite dog since 1991 for good reason: they're good ol' boys who are just as much at home riding in the cab of a pickup truck as curled up in the parlor of your country estate. These sporting dogs will fetch a ball (or a duck), and do it all day, especially if deep water is involved. Working retriever, guide dog, service dog, contraband detector—they set the standard for every job, but excel especially at being everyday companions. They're playful, energetic, gregarious, and smart. But they're big, about 55 to 80 pounds (25–36 kg), and powerful, and they can drag you down the street unless you train them (and sometimes, even when you've trained them). Usually, they'll just drag you to meet the next person they see; there's nothing snobbish about a Lab. They come in black, brown, and all shades of yellow. A proud parent of the Australian and the American Labradoodles (featured on pages 57 and 89, respectively), the Lab also shares its good genes with the Labbe (page 51), the Labmaraner (page 69), and the Chesador (page 115).

Cocker Spaniel Chase a ball, seek out a bird, make a new friend—all in a day's fun for the sporting dog dubbed the "merry" American. The Cocker Spaniel comes in two versions, English and American, and the American Cocker comes in three varieties: black, parti (spotted), or ASCOB (which stands for Any Solid Color Other than Black). American Cockers held the place as America's most popular breed for more than two decades. That might be partly because they can wag their tails until they vibrate at ultrasonic speed, and they'll do it at the slightest provocation. They're kind of obedient—at least, they try, unless something else distracts them, like a leaf falling. Get a Cocker focused, though, and he'll try his heart out for you. They wear their coat like a royal cape but, without lots of upkeep, that cape can turn into a crown of thorns and coat of rags. They weigh from 24 to 28 pounds (11–13 kg). The Cocker Spaniel makes up half of the parentage of one of the most popular hybrids, the Cockapoo (featured on page 45), as well as the Comfort Retriever (page 41), and the Cockalier (page 119).

Socialite

All-American Boy

Cavalier King Charles Spaniel Here's a hint: they come from a family originally known as "comforter spaniels," and that's exactly what they do. Among the gentlest of toy breeds, Cavaliers have been comforting and enchanting royal families for centuries, warming laps, feet, and hearts. In the eighteenth century, King Charles II was so smitten with his comforter spaniels that he was accused of ignoring state matters so he could be with his dogs. That's a problem with Cavaliers; they're so much fun, so affectionate, so willing to please, that it's hard to tear yourself away. They're friends to all, and to know a Cavalier is to love one. But they do have spaniel in those genes, and once outside, they love to explore and hunt—even if it's just chasing a butterfly. Cavaliers weigh between 13 and 18 pounds (6–8 kg), and come in four color patterns: solid red, red and white, black and tan, and tricolor (black, tan, and white). The Cavalier King Charles Spaniel's most popular hybrid is the Cavachon (featured on page 25), along with the Cavapoo (page 85) and the Cockalier (page 119).

Jack Russell Terrier There's a reason people call them Jack Russell Terrorists. Terriers in general have a reputation for being boisterous and rascally, but these pranksters set the bar. The Jack Russell is a doer, not a thinker, and he rushes in where only fools and terriers dare. He'll attack your pillows until a flurry of goose down floats to the floor, and before it can settle he'll be off to bark out the window or get outside to tunnel under the fence—he's got places to go, people to see, and mischief to stir up. This willingness to try anything twice and to be creatively bad is what makes them both gifted animal actors and, too often, drop-offs at the shelter. You need to spend lots of time with these impetuous dogs to give their urges an outlet. Jack Russells tend to weigh in between 13 and 17 pounds (6–8 kg). Their coats come with wiry, smooth, or broken (that's sort of in-between) textures, and mixtures of white, black, and brown colors. Hybrid offspring seem to inherit their zest for life (and trouble). Examples include the Jackabee (featured on 97), the Jackapoo (page 109), and the Jack Chi (page 127).

Designer Dogs

activeness	●●●○○
barking	●●○○○
dog friendliness	●●●●●
grooming	●●●●●
people friendliness	●●●●●
shedding	●●○○○
trainability	●●●●○

Cavachon

With her perfect coif and winsome wiles, the Cavachon seems like a surefire favorite at the debutante ball—but this pretty princess is anything but prim. Toss her a squeak toy, and she'll go from graceful to goofy in two seconds flat.

The Cavachon is one dog who definitely blends the best traits of both her parents. She comes from two fashion-conscious breeds, the Cavalier King Charles Spaniel and the Bichon Frise, and she mixes the Cavalier's traditional sweet innocence with the Bichon's bouncy style. Flirty, perky, and a little edgy, the Cavachon makes cute look cool, while winning you over with her irrepressible cheer.

With a blink of her big round eyes, a toss of her luscious locks, and a hearty wag of her tail, she knows she can get what she wants. She may turn on the Cavachon charm, climbing in your lap with a wiggle and a lick, or she may go for laughs, with a wave of her paw and a cock of her head. She loves her creature comforts, but she's no gold digger; she means it when she says she loves you (though a new diamond collar could help her love you more!).

She's more of a city gal than a nature lover, and is completely at home roaming an apartment or penthouse. But she does need to get plenty of exercise every day—a pup must stay fit, you know.

Fortunately, a Cavachon is always ready to get out of the house and visit with her many friends, both canine and human (and even feline), so it's not difficult to make sure she's getting a good workout. Especially fond of children, this prima playmate frolics with them with abandon. (What child could resist a fluffy friend that looks like a plush animal?)

But don't be fooled by her doll-like looks. She can't be treated like a plaything or a fashion accessory. She thrives on attention and can't handle being ignored. But given the exercise and regard she's entitled to, she is a gracious house dog, and not so big on barking (it's really so beneath her).

Cavachons weigh between 15 and 25 pounds (7–12 kg). They're seen in white, peach, red, sable, or black and tan, either solid or on a white background. Spotted Cavachons often have the symmetrically patched facial pattern of the Cavalier. Their coats are long, slightly wavy to curly, and, breeders claim, hypoallergenic. Though their coats are low-shedding, they will require daily brushing.

activeness	●●●●●
barking	●●●●○
dog friendliness	●●●●●
grooming	●●●○○
people friendliness	●●●●●
shedding	●●○○○
trainability	●●●●●

Papipoo

Gifted with genius and geniality, the Papipoo is always up for a round of playful punditry. Whether she's figuring the rate at which a dog treat drops or yapping about the latest pup fiction, life with this thinker is no trivial pursuit.

The child of two success-driven parents, the toy Papillon and the sporty Poodle, this dog's good sense (and good looks) come naturally. When a Papipoo claims she's smarter than the average dog, she's being humble—she's really a canine Einstein.

Part philosopher, part amateur scientist, she has an undying curiosity. Give her a new toy, and she'll play with it for a while. Then she'll take it apart so she can study its tensile properties. Try to sneak generic dog food into her bowl and she'll detect the deception right off. And don't even think about trying to fool her by spelling things out, even in a whisper. Those trademark Papillon ears catch it all.

She's a savvy gal who knows it takes more than brains and beauty to get ahead. She can schmooze with the best of them, but she's not just playing politics; she really is a people person—er, puppy. With a proffered paw, a tilt of her head, and an understanding yip, she has that rare ability to make everyone she meets feel special, like a long-lost friend or a newfound confidante.

It's her people-pleasing aspect that makes a Papipoo so much fun to live with. She's a show-off at heart, and loves to learn tricks that can amaze your friends. And don't think she won't speak up if you don't take advantage of her brain power. A Papipoo without a job to do or tasks to learn can become frustrated at being an underachiever.

And don't call her a "pet" or a "dog." She's one of the family, almost human, and she'll be insulted if she's not treated as an equal—or better. She expects to be a part of daily life, and will protest eloquently if she's not. A Papipoo also knows that an active body is the best way to feed an active mind, so she insists on working out every day.

Papipoos stay trim, weighing 6 to 12 pounds (3–5 kg), so they're small enough to tote around in a doggy purse—but don't be surprised if they insist on navigating. They come in many colors, mostly blacks and reds, both solid and spotted. Their coats are generally long and wavy, with a smart bounce, and need brushing every other day.

activeness ●●●●○
barking ●●●●○
dog friendliness ●○○○○
grooming ●○○○○
people friendliness ●●○○○
shedding ●○○○○
trainability ●●●○○

Chiweenie

Favoring her Latin parent, the Chiweenie likes life with a dash of salsa. This cha-cha chica will keep you tangoing through the day, trying to keep up with her tiny two-step. But when she slows down, she's as sweet as dulce de leche.

Part saucy Chihuahua, part peppy Dachshund, the Chiweenie is a spicy blend that's hot, hot, hot! She's a zesty dog that follows her own sense of style and fun, the chili pepper of designer dogs. Anybody who dares dance with her better keep in step.

Chiweenies are bold, bright, and full of bluster. Actually, the bluster isn't all that bright when it comes to mouthing off at bigger dogs, which she may tend to do, but that's OK—you're there to shield her from her own delusions of grandeur, pulling her to safety as she barks the canine equivalent of "Hold me back!" at that Pit Bull. (Chiweenies have a bit of a Napoleon complex.) But it's all in a day's roller-coaster ride for a cocky Chiweenie in search of her next big kick.

Like a coming-of-age teen, she's independent, headstrong, and pretty sure she knows more than you. A brainy type who uses her smarts to get what she wants, this persuasive pooch will have her way by any means, whether going for the sympathy vote or the laughs. She's a city dog, with tenement attitude but town-house tastes. The Chiweenie learns fast, and enjoys showing off her repertoire of tricks. A great watchdog, she'll announce the arrival of visitors and make sure they're on the guest list.

This mambo mama is a thrill seeker, so she won't be happy hanging out at home. Sure, she can run back and forth from room to room to exercise her body, but she needs lots of mental stimulation, too—not to mention a chance to learn some new moves. She's a do-it-yourself dog who prefers to get around on her own four legs, and won't be content to ride in a doggy purse for long (unless that purse is going someplace exciting where she'd otherwise get stepped on). Her hound-dog heritage may occasionally drive her to follow her nose and go on a hunt, so take care when allowing her off leash.

Chiweenies love playing with children, but at 5 to 15 pounds (2–7 kg), some may be too small for toddlers to handle. They're seen in fawn, black and tan, chocolate, red, brindle, merle, and spotted, and in smooth- or long-coated varieties.

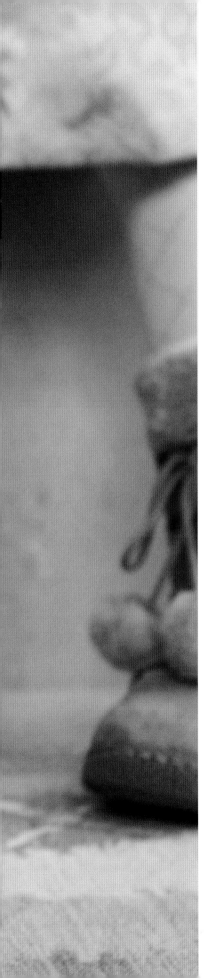

Lhasapoo

Although she looks fluffy as a meringue, the Lhasapoo is much more than a frivolous little puppy. Known as much for her tough-girl temperament as for her endearing appearance, she's a steadfast sweetheart and a friend for life.

Sure, a Lhasapoo seems like an innocent puffball, but look out! This little darling is a tough character, a guard dog masquerading as a luxe lapdog. Thanks to her Lhasa Apso parent, whose original Tibetan name translates to "Bark Lion Sentinel Dog," she's bold beyond her size. True, a Lhasapoo won't exactly be able to bring down a purse-snatcher, but she'll sound the alarm and make a good show of protecting you. (Just don't dare trying to tell her that she's actually not a lion.)

In truth, she's a total glamour-puss, and nothing is too bright and bold for this pup. She's also a bit lofty, with a look-but-don't-touch attitude. Her real affection is reserved for only a special few, and when she gives her heart, she gives it all. But even so, she's not one for showy displays of affection.

She's smart, but she doesn't flaunt it (she'd rather outfox you just when you least suspect it). In fact, she may spend twice as much energy figuring out how to creatively disobey you than to simply comply with your silly commands. But she knows

when she's got it good, so make it worth her while, and she'll be eating out of your hand and behaving as well as her good-girl appearance would suggest.

No matter her age, she'll always seem young at heart, and she frisks and frolics with abandon. But don't expect her to fetch. Please. She'd rather just run and romp, or promenade down the lane. She's an active pooch, a firm believer in exercise, and she'll give you a piece of her mind if you don't get her out and about. (Come to think of it, she doesn't mind giving her opinion freely about pretty much everything, and does so whenever the world doesn't hew to the Lhasapoo outlook on life.)

As glam as she is, she's actually a tad heavy, weighing about 12 to 17 pounds (5–8 kg), but she carries it well. The Lhasapoo coat palette is among the more varied: white (pictured here), cream (page 37), sable, and black, are all common, in bright solids or bold patterns. Those lovely Lhasapoo locks are long and lush, and low shedding, but are high-maintenance, so they'll require daily brushing.

activeness	●●○○○
barking	●●●●○
dog friendliness	●●●●●
grooming	●●○○○
people friendliness	●●●●●
shedding	●●●○○
trainability	●●○○○

Bagle Hound

This easygoing guy doesn't sweat the small stuff—or the big stuff, for that matter. With his lowrider build and hang-loose outlook, the Bagle Hound is as cool as they come, and as relaxing as a nap on a summer lawn.

This dog is a dude who's decidedly down home. An agreeable blend of two ol' hound dogs, the fairly energetic Beagle and the much more mellow Basset Hound, the Bagle Hound is a laid-back canine who likes to lounge about and watch the sun rise and set over the lawn, eating and playing in the sunshine, but mostly following the shade.

Of course, that's when he's grown up. A younger Bagle Hound is almost the exact opposite: a restless adventurer in search of a way off the farm, certain that greener pastures and better scents lie on the other side of the field, or fence, or street. He's a pillaging pirate out to plunder your cabinets, an explorer in search of buried treasure he may find in your backyard (or laundry basket).

If a Bagle Hound described his ideal day, it would be: a run in the woods, a nap, a big meal, a nap, a chance to cuddle—and nap, time to eat again, and bedtime. Sleeping, eating, loving, and hunting pretty much define a Bagle Hound's priorities. Oh, and napping. Did we mention napping?

The Bagle Hound is a happy-go-lucky fellow who lives for the moment and scrounges up whatever he can find. On the rare occasions he does volunteer for work, he'll maybe sign up as a field and fishing guide (just be careful he doesn't eat the bait). Like both his parent breeds, the chance to hunt awakens his primal instincts (but then, his instincts to snack and sleep might win out instead).

In terms of obedience, he tends to have an "I'll-get-back-to-you-on-that" attitude. If you try to insist that there are consequences to that mindset, he'll generally follow up with a wag of the tail and lick of the tongue that says "What—me worry?" Usually he will work for food, though. (Well, that's if he's in the mood and the stars are aligned. But then he also may just bay at the moon, and he's really loud.)

He's big, around 30 to 50 pounds (12–23 kg), but he doesn't throw his weight around. He usually wears patterns of white, brown, black, and lemon, and, as befits his style, his coat care is minimal, so you won't have to fret about this guy's fashion.

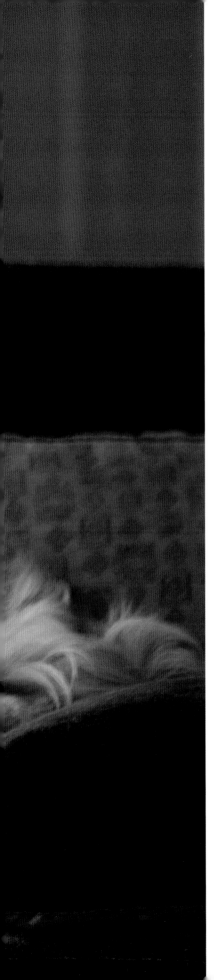

activeness	●●●○○
barking	●●●○○
dog friendliness	●●●●●
grooming	●●●○○
people friendliness	●●●●●
shedding	●●●○○
trainability	●●●●●

Comfort Retriever

Whether luxuriating on a velvety perch or romping up a storm outside, the Comfort Retriever is the apple of every dog lover's eye. With her satiny coat and sweet nature, she's the perfect personification of her hybrid moniker.

"If only Golden Retrievers came in a smaller size!" That was the thought behind the Comfort Retriever, the product of crossing a Golden Retriever with a Cocker Spaniel (either American or English). Also known as "Cogols" or "Golden Cockers," somehow "Comfort Retriever" seems more apt a name, because touching one almost immediately gives you an overwhelming feeling of, well, comfort.

This popular pup is an instant friend, and she isn't particularly picky about her social set. She'll be buddies with practically anyone she meets, greeting them like long-lost family, be they dog, cat, or gate-crasher. In the eyes of a Comfort Retriever, everyone is innocent until proven guilty—especially if they'll toss a stick! And, if they offer her the chance to go for a swim, she'll give them a pledge of lifetime allegiance. It's not that this good-natured chum is oblivious to our shortcomings; in fact, she's one of the smartest dogs around. She just prefers to see the best in people, and ends up bringing out the best in them as a result. Spend a little time with her, and you're bound to leave in a better mood.

A Comfort Retriever demands that you perk up and pay attention, and lots of it, in exchange for her loyalty. That includes lots of outdoor adventures. Although she's smaller and easier to exercise than a full-size Golden, she's not going to do well in an apartment unless it has a doggie gym or some other outlet for exertion. It's not that she's hyperactive—she just can't bear being cooped up unless you tire her out, physically and mentally, every day. Fortunately, she's likely to be gifted when it comes to learning things, so time spent training usually results in impressive feats.

Physically, Comfort Retrievers resemble the Golden parent more than the Cocker, but with longer ears and a lighter build, growing to about 35 pounds (16 kg). They come in shades of gold and black, and are always solid. The coat is soft and silky, like that of a Golden Retriever (though breeders claim they shed less). To maintain her deluxe looks, you'll need to brush her twice a week. But given how comforting it is to be in contact with her, you may even want to do it more often!

activeness	●●●●○
barking	●●●○○
dog friendliness	●●●●●
grooming	●●●●●
people friendliness	●●●●●
shedding	●●○○○
trainability	●●●●○

Cockapoo

Since well before anyone called him a "designer dog," the Cockapoo has been a consistent crowd-pleaser—and for good reason. He combines all the most attractive attributes of his parents into one irresistible bundle of love.

The Cockapoo is the little black dress of the designer-dog world—he never goes out of style. This versatile star has been around for more than forty years, and he's more popular now than ever. As chic as he is charming, he's big-dog enough to go hiking, but little-dog enough to tuck in a lap (well, maybe a large lap). Factor in a luxuriant low-shedding, low-allergy coat that may be silky, curly, or cut short like a stylish mouton, and you've got a top-notch design that's always in fashion.

As with all classics, personality plays an important part in his appeal. A combination of two all-time favorite family dogs, the Cocker Spaniel and the Poodle, the Cockapoo is just what you'd expect: smart, fun-loving, affectionate, gentle, and always so very happy to see you. You want to take a nap? He's there. Throw a ball? He'll fetch. Go on a roadtrip? He's on board. Take a walk? He'll get the leash. At home on a rural farm or in a city flat, and as good with children as he is with adults, a Cockapoo is happy almost anywhere, doing almost anything, as long as he's with his family.

Cockapoos are active dogs that need to exercise their minds and bodies every day. They learn quickly and enjoy showing off how clever they are. A Cockapoo also hungers for your recognition. If you don't give it to him freely, he'll remind you by following you around and getting underfoot. If that doesn't work, he may resort to redecorating your house. That should get your attention.

The Cockapoo's design allows for more variations than most. Though usually a Miniature, the Poodle parent may also be a Toy or Standard, and the Cocker Spaniel parent may be English but is usually American. They come in three sizes: Toy (under 12 pounds/5 kg), Miniature (13–20 pounds/6–9 kg), and Standard (over 20 pounds/9 kg), and in enough hues to make a Hollywood hairstylist jealous. Their coats can be spotted or solid, in black, gray, white (pages 48–49), brown, or red, just for starters. Famous for their soft and touchable fur, their coats range from wavy to curly. As with all beauty, theirs comes with a cost: Cockapoos need to be brushed every day and clipped every six to eight weeks.

activeness	●●●●○
barking	●●●○○
dog friendliness	●●●●●
grooming	●●○○○
people friendliness	●●●●●
shedding	●●●○○
trainability	●●●●○

Labbe

This bold buddy takes on the world by leaps and bounds. Spring-loaded and ready for action, the Labbe chases anything that moves and fetches balls like his life depended on it—why do you think they call him a "retriever"?

"Life partner wanted. Must like hunting, fishing, long walks on the beach, and long nights by the fire. Wrestling a plus." Post an ad like this, and your in-box will be full of replies—from Labbes (also known as Beagadors). They're the product of a cross between two consummate sports lovers, the Labrador Retriever and the Beagle.

A friend to all, the Labbe trails genuine hospitality behind him wherever he goes. He'll give you a wag of his tail and a slurp of his tongue, and he'll lend a paw when he can. He'll even give you his ball, if you promise to throw it (and throw it and throw it).

This fetching fellow has his own style, but it's one you won't see on any Paris runway. He's a working-class dog, so he's the type who'd favor plaids, hunter orange, or even camouflage. On dry land, he'd prefer to be seen in a customized truck, decked out with lots of chrome and coated in mud. Also at home in the water, he'd be happy to sail the seas in a tricked-out motor boat—powered with high horsepower, of course, just like he is.

The Labbe's dream job? Hunting guide. He'd spend every day in the field if he could, following a trail or diving in after a bird. If there's nothing to hunt, he'll settle for tearing around. In short, he's no city slicker and may not be so happy spending his days in an apartment or pounding urban pavement as he would be in a big yard or running rural byways.

He's stubborn to a fault, so you might have a hard time convincing him to go shopping or to a cafe. He'd rather spend his time at a backyard barbecue than at a fancy restaurant. But feed him well and you'll win him over wherever you go. In truth, despite his occasional obstinacy, the Labbe's a total sweetheart. He has no problem with public displays of affection (there's that tongue again), and he's not picky about who he gets affectionate with.

Labbes tend to be hefty guys, usually weighing in anywhere between 30 and 50 pounds (14–23 kg). They wear a thick, short coat, which comes in all shades of yellow, from light cream to strawberry blond, and are seen, rarely, in chocolate.

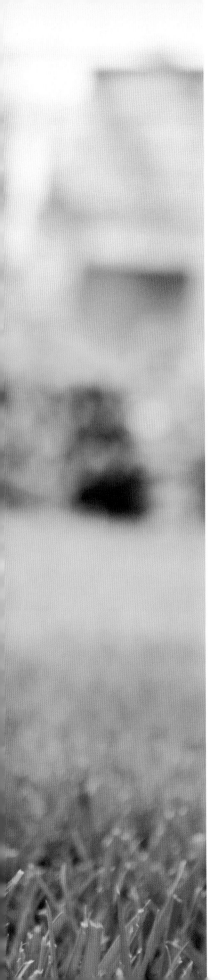

activeness	●●●●○
barking	●●●●○
dog friendliness	●●●○○
grooming	●●●●●
people friendliness	●●●●○
shedding	●●○○○
trainability	●●●○○

Yorkipoo

Don't let this Lilliputian fool you—the Yorkipoo is a tiny tyke with big-time charisma, and enough moxie to take on strangers six times her size. But though she can be devilish, she's also angelic, and as clever as she is cuddly.

Meet the Yorkipoo, one of the most diminutive designer dogs. She's the perfect size for tucking under an arm or in a bag for a day of shopping and salon-ing. But beware: she won't be content to just sit on the sidelines. This gregarious little gremlin likes to mix it up in the middle of things, and she'll feel put out if she's not the center of attention.

The Yorkipoo has an inflated sense of self, an opinion she won't hesitate to let you in on, but this only adds to her mischievous appeal. The mix of Terrier pluck and Poodle smarts makes for the kind of friend your mother warned you about: one who's always coming up with novel ways of getting into trouble. She knows she can cock her head just so, add a few apologetic licks, and not only will she get away with chewing the heels off your new Manolo Blahniks, she'll also have you taking a photo to show everyone how cute she was doing it. Luckily, even Yorkipoos get tired, and after a day of barking, schmoozing, and directing everyone around her, she'll become the picture of innocence as she snuggles close and steals your heart.

Alert and clever, the Yorkipoo is a quick learner when she focuses her energy on being good, so the main challenge is convincing her that being good pays off. Given a satisfactory pay rate, she's highly trainable and excels at picking up tricks.

Strongly family oriented, she's good with gentle children, but she's too small and frisky for very young children to handle safely without close supervision. She also makes a great apartment dog, with one caveat: if she can't go outside to work out her body and mind, she may instead choose to regularly exercise her voice.

Yorkipoos weigh only about 4 to 10 pounds (2–5 kg). In contrast to the Yorkshire Terrier's single choice of color scheme, Yorkipoos can be found in a full spectrum of colors, courtesy of their Poodle parentage. Popular hues include black and tan, apricot, black, silver, and white. Their coats shed only slightly and may be better for people with allergies, but they do require daily brushing—after all, a Yorkipoo must always look her very best.

activeness	●●●●○
barking	●●○○○
dog friendliness	●●●●●
grooming	●●●●●
people friendliness	●●●●●
shedding	●●○○○
trainability	●●●●○

Australian Labradoodle

One of the first breeds on the designer-dog scene, this fella has rocketed his way to international stardom. Whether you're up for some Aussie rules football, or just snuggling and having a cuppa, this bloke's always game.

The land Down Under used to be best known for kangaroos and boomerangs, but that was before the Australian Labradoodle wagged his tail onto the scene. This dinky di pooch isn't your average designer dog. In fact, he's technically not a standard hybrid. He started off as a simple cross of a Labrador Retriever and a Poodle, but then the recipe got complicated. A dash of Irish Water Spaniel, a dollop of Curly-Coated Retriever, and a sprinkling of English and American Cocker Spaniels went into the mix. Now the breed has worldwide clubs, such as the International Labradoodle Association, working to promote the Australian Labradoodle as a legitimate breed-in-development.

Greeting everyone with tail-wag semaphore for "G'day, mate," Aussie Labradoodles are friends to all, more likely to invite a burglar in to fire up the barbie than they are to scare him away. If you have a game to play or a walkabout to take, he's an instant chum. He may even dazzle you with his "kangadoodle," a vertical jump that launches him up among the stars—where he belongs, of course.

Once back on the ground, he's equally athletic and energetic, and loves to run, swim, and fetch. Great in the outdoors, this 'Doodle is less suited to the city (unless you can devote your entire life to running and throwing balls). But he's more than a star jock. He's smart and actually likes having a job to do. He's a gifted retriever, an enthusiastic obedience dog, and a successful service dog. In fact, he was first developed as a guide dog for the blind.

Breeders have created Australian Labradoodles in three sizes: Standard (50–65 pounds/23–30 kg); Medium (30–45 pounds/13–20 kg); and Miniature (15–25 pounds/7–12 kg). They come in a variety of stylish coat types and colors (most of which need to be groomed every couple of days). Their coats can be wool, which hangs in loose spirals and needs clipping; fleece, which is silky and wavy; or hair, which doesn't require as much grooming but does shed and has odor. Solid chocolate, black, gray, cream, and red are colors seen most often. But no matter what kind of coat he wears, an Australian Labradoodle is a true-blue pal.

activeness	●●●●●
barking	●●●●○
dog friendliness	●●○○○
grooming	●○○○○
people friendliness	●●●○○
shedding	●○○○○
trainability	●●○○○

Toy Fox Pinscher

One glimpse of this fellow's princely prance, and you'll know the Toy Fox Pinscher is a breed apart. What may come as a surprise is his turbo timing: he expects everything to happen lickety-split. On your mark, get set, go!

The Toy Fox Pinscher is dogdom's version of a perpetual motion machine, always revved and ready to go. A high-voltage cross of the busy-busy Miniature Pinscher and the hyped-up Toy Fox Terrier, the Toy Fox Pinscher is, in a word, amped.

Throw your alarm clock away. No need for one with a dog that greets you before dawn with a pounce on your chest and a face full of kisses. He'll follow you around, urging you to come on, get going, he has a busy schedule ahead! He has toys to torment, cats to chase, leaves to bark at, places to go, and people to meet. Why aren't you up yet?

If you're lucky, you can grab a cup of coffee on your way out the door for his morning walk. And you'll need it if you expect to keep up. He may be small, but his ideas aren't, and he won't be satisfied if his exercise is just a tiny trek around the block.

He likes to explore, but he can be too adventurous for his own good, so you can't let him off leash unless he's in a safe and secure area. He's actually a varmint hunter at heart and, like his terrier ancestors, he relishes the chance to get down and dirty in search of hapless rodents. He love games and the people (especially kids) who play them.

Warning: this toy terror can be rowdy around other dogs, and he'll often start fracases he has no hope of winning. You can try carrying him in a doggy purse to keep him out of trouble, but don't expect him to sit still for too long. Oh, don't worry—he actually does sleep, eventually. And when he does, he likes a warm lap to snooze in.

As for obedience? Um, don't hold your breath. This lad is smart, and he'll quickly master tricks, but he's highly distractible and not into following orders. He loves to hear himself bark, and makes an ideal watchdog (if you don't mind a few false alarms).

At 4 to 10 pounds (2–5 kg), the Toy Fox Pinscher is a true lightweight. His coat is soft and silky, and is most often seen in black and tan, chocolate, sable, red, and tan, all with or without white markings.

activeness	●●●○○
barking	●●○○○
dog friendliness	●●●●●
grooming	●●●●●
people friendliness	●●●●●
shedding	●●○○○
trainability	●●●●○

Goldendoodle

This laid-back dog breezes onto every scene with a good-natured "woof!" and a trademark high-five. Robust and a bit of a tomboy, she's also an intuitive people-pleaser, and she's sure to make friends wherever she goes.

The Goldendoodle's great popularity is entirely understandable. She's a dog with an at-your-service attitude, and she's happiest hanging out with her buddies and making new friends. She'll bend over backward to bring a smile to your face, and will do everything in her power to give you whatever you want. With her chipper, bowl-half-full outlook, she's always up for palling around, whether escorting you to the sofa or jogging alongside you across a park.

Her Poodle parent is a city dog with country roots, but her Golden Retriever parent makes no such pretense—he's unrepentantly rustic. So she's equally at home in a limousine or pickup truck, and she's too self-assured to be snobbish about her style. She's not ashamed to wear a bandanna, and she's fine with you wearing a baseball cap.

This cordial kid gets along with all she meets: cats, dogs, total strangers—everyone is a potential pal. She especially enjoys playing with children, or with anyone else who shares her sense of fun. She's a speedy learner, and loves to show off her tricks.

Her sporting-dog heritage makes her a natural-born fetcher and swimmer, and that's how she prefers to get her exercise, so a Goldendoodle is best suited to suburban or country life. And she does need a workout. Deprive her of the chance to tire herself out, and she may direct her energy toward mischief.

But a Goldendoodle can adapt to city life, too. She does cut a fine figure strolling along Main Street. Just remember: in her heart she's pulling for the park and the chance to chase ducks. To make urban life work well for her, this active girl will need access to open fields and ponds, and room to run.

Goldendoodles usually have a Standard Poodle parent. Females weigh between 45 and 65 pounds (20–29 kg), while males tend to come in at a heftier 55–90 pounds (25–41 kg). Fewer Goldendoodles have a Miniature Poodle parent, but those that do weigh about 25–45 pounds (11–20 kg). Their coats may be cream, gold, apricot, chocolate, gray, or black, and often resemble relaxed spiral curls, growing to about 4 to 7 inches (10–18 cm) in length.

activeness ●●●●●
barking ●●●○○
dog friendliness ●●●●○
grooming ●●○○○
people friendliness ●●●●●
shedding ●●○○○
trainability ●●●○○

Labmaraner

Sleek and agile, the Labmaraner craves a sprint on the beach or a scurry down the block, especially if the grand finish is in your arms. In the dash for zesty fun, this track star bolts full speed ahead—and gets your pulse racing, too.

The Labmaraner's a dog who's definitely at home on the run. Her parents, a Labrador Retriever and a Weimaraner, both love the outdoors, and she not only followed in their paw prints, she also ran on ahead. There's no holding back a Labmaraner!

She yearns for wide open spaces where she can race with wild abandon, sucking in fresh air and stirring up sand. If she flushes out a few seagulls along the way, so much the better—hope they can move fast. Hope you can move fast, too, because once she shifts into Labmaraner high gear, she may not stop running until she reaches the horizon.

There's not a pretentious bone in her body, and her style is decidedly casual. To dress her up, a sporty collar will do (with a racing-stripe motif, of course), and a matching towel might also come in handy after a particularly vigorous jog. She's also an extremely friendly sort, the kind who's willing to share her water bottle with every dog or person she meets (she may not be so generous with cats). As loving as she is lively, she's very demonstrative.

Early training is essential for this cross-country pro, although learning isn't her favorite thing. She can be easily distracted unless you give her a more rewarding reason to pay attention. She just needs the right motivation—often a mix of tasty rewards and tough regulations. Even so, when she's young, she can be impetuous, stubborn, and downright untamed. This dog's an athlete in the making, so she may need a little, well, making.

She's not a city dog at heart, so if you're an urbanite you'll need to arrange lots of playdates and park visits for her, and even in the country she'll need a lot of activity to keep her from using your home as an obstacle course. Plenty of runs, games, and lessons will prevent you from having to bench her. Active children are favorite playmates (and are perfect since they can match her endless energy).

Labmaraners are both tall and heavy, ranging in weight from 50 to 100 pounds (23–45 kg). Their short coats come in all shades of yellow from dark gold to pale cream, black, and chocolate.

activeness ●●●○○
barking ●●●○○
dog friendliness ●●●○○
grooming ●●●●●
people friendliness ●●●○○
shedding ●○○○○
trainability ●●●●○

Tibetoodle

Serene, pensive, and a bit enigmatic, the Tibetoodle is the mystic of the dog realm. His wise eyes and fuzzy form win fans wherever he goes, but he stays slightly above the fray, and practices a Zen approach to daily life.

An inspired blend of the Tibetan Terrier and the Poodle, the Tibetoodle is a dog with many layers to his personality. His Tibetan side comes from stock bred in Buddhist monasteries centuries ago, where they were raised as family companions who might occasionally help with chores, but who weren't bred for work. His Poodle side adds smarts and charm to his inscrutability, creating an irresistible mix.

He's a somewhat private fellow, most comfortable at home with his inner circle, but not exactly shy when he's out on the town. Though by now he's used to being the center of attention, he just doesn't crave it as some do. He'd rather save his best moments for his special people in the privacy of home, where he can just hang loose and be himself, alternately clowning and lounging around.

But he needs far more than that to feel fulfilled in life. He needs to meditate, walk, and explore, and to run free and frolic. He also enjoys the company of other dogs, and even cats—after all, his Tibetan Buddhist heritage makes him a lover of all life.

The Tibetoodle needs things to do and he loves getting places under his own paw power. In fact, he demands a lot of exercise, and he'll be unhappy if you drive him everywhere. He also likes to exercise his brain, so learning is a favorite pastime. (He may even be able to teach you a trick or two.) But once this keen canine has satisfied his urge to perform, he'll prove that he's a lover of lounging as well, and after a day well spent, he's content to share his couch with you and take in some vintage flicks.

On the other side, he does get into trouble once in a while—what freethinker doesn't? He's been known to try his hand at Feng Shui, rearranging things as he sees fit, if he's left too long on his own. But usually he's quick to learn the rules that count, and he generally aims to please. (A few bribes along the way never hurt, though.)

Tibetoodles weigh 15 to 24 pounds (7–11 kg). Their long coats may be kept long and flying free, or carefully clipped and coiffed. They come in many colors and need to be brushed three times a week.

activeness	●●●○○
barking	●●●●○
dog friendliness	●●●○○
grooming	●●●○○
people friendliness	●●●○○
shedding	●●○○○
trainability	●●●○○

Doxiepoo

A mini maestro with headliner allure, the Doxiepoo sure knows how to appeal to the masses. But he's no fly-by-night fad. Let this little Liberace play you a song, and you'll be filling his tip jar every night—with doggy treats, of course.

He dances to a different drummer, boogies to his own beat. He's the Doxiepoo, half Dachshund, half Poodle (also called a Doodle), and he's one-of-a-kind when it comes to expressing himself—the next Ameri-canine Idol. And what he may sometimes lack in talent he makes up for in style and pluck.

This dog is graced with many gifts. He'll bark out a staccato verse and follow it with a howling love song. He'll dance with delight when it's time to go for a walk. He has no problem learning the routines; he's a quick study and can bust a move or pick up tricks like a pro. With a cock of his head, he'll have fans clamoring for his attention. Yes, he's a bit of a ham, but it's all part of the Doxiepoo charm.

The truth is, he's really a pretty private guy when it comes right down to it. He prefers to meet folks one on one, and likes to get to know them before opening up. His inner circle is small, but once you make it in, he's ready to stick by you through fame and fortune, failure and famine, and he's as loving a pal as you're likely to find.

His true love is kids, and he'll abandon all pretense and play like a puppy with those he knows. As far as other dogs, he makes up his mind about them one at a time. He's a little guy, and can get himself into a pickle trying to stand up to other pooches.

His Dachshund genes drive him to hound around more than his prissy Poodle part would care to admit. Look, just because he's an artist doesn't mean he doesn't also have a talent for trouble. He likes to try some tomfoolery whenever he has a chance (it adds a little flair to his nice-guy image), and outdoor adventures are among his favorite things, thanks to his Dachshund parentage.

This pocket-sized pooch usually weighs between 8 and 20 pounds (4–9 kg). He'll wear his hair in almost any style (it can be long and wavy or shorter and wiry), and just about any color goes, solid or spotted. Common colors include merle, black and tan, red, and black. If he's wiry, you'll want to brush him weekly, but if he has longer, wavy hair, he'll need attention two or three times a week.

activeness	●●●●○
barking	●●●●○
dog friendliness	●●●●●
grooming	●●●●○
people friendliness	●●●●●
shedding	●●○○○
trainability	●●●○○

Poogle

Rough-and-tumble but also urbane, the Poogle is a slapstick kid with mighty magnetism. While this swell guy is known for his sly jesting and spry smarts, you'll also adore him for his gung-ho enthusiasm and easy affection.

The Poogle is a pup with a bit of an identity crisis. He's part city slicker, part country classic, decidedly dashing but slightly doggy. That's what happens when a sophisticated Poodle and a down-to-earth Beagle get together. The result is a pooch who flits between folksy and hoity-toity with hardly a hitch, hightailing it after a scent in the park and then making a break for downtown to scope out the scene and mingle with the adoring masses.

And speaking of devoted fans, this friendly fellow has legions, winning pals galore with his jovial personality and his fondness for fun, not to mention his prankster ways. He's likely to nab your shoe and hide it under the bed, flashing his hallmark look of innocence when he's found out. But hey, he's such a good buddy, who minds a missing sneaker or two?

He loves to visit the city, but he probably won't take much of a shine to high-rise living. This populist pup is a good ol' boy through and through, and he'll only tolerate putting on city airs for so long. Oh, he'll say hello to passersby (he never met a human

he didn't like) and he'll be happy to join you at an uptown cafe. But his real love is to head out to the country, where he can go swimming and hunting and gleefully roughhouse with you and his other friends. He's also at home in the suburbs, carpooling to soccer practice (or the obedience academy) and hanging out at block parties.

This guy is exuberant and gregarious, a dog about town with backwoods ease. Have kids? He's one at heart. Other dogs? He'll deal them in, do some partying, and get them baying along with him, karaoke style. (You're invited to join, too.)

Depending on the size of the Poodle parent, a Poogle may weigh from 15 to 45 pounds (7–20 kg). (Though yours may often urge you to pull over at the fast-food drive-through, watch the fatty foods. Poogles can struggle to keep their weight down.) As for style, he wears his wavy hair tousled, in colors of cream, brown, red, black, or gray, either solid or patched. He should be brushed every other day, and if his hair is longer, clipped occasionally.

activeness	●●●○○
barking	●●○○○
dog friendliness	●●●○○
grooming	●●○○○
people friendliness	●●○○○
shedding	●●●○○
trainability	●●●○○

Frenchie Pug

You might think you'd go cruising for a bruising with a Frenchie Pug, with his tough-guy stance and steely stare. In fact, this cute brute is a lover, not a fighter, and he'll win your heart with his wrinkled kisser and playful personality.

Chunky, funky, and fun—that's the Frenchie Pug, and it shouldn't be a surprise, since this pooch is half pudgy Pug, half frisky French Bulldog. Both breeds are known for their frolicsome ways, full figures, and flat faces, and the Frenchie Pug follows suit.

Behind that gargoyle smile lurks the heart of a clown. Whether it's wrestling an imaginary foe, pretending to eavesdrop on your conversation (and maybe even joining in with a few well-placed woofs), or smothering you with French kisses, his day isn't done until he's pried a smile from your lips.

With his Mastiff and Bulldog roots, the Frenchie Pug can't help being stubborn. That means most attempts to "show him who's boss" will usually leave you on the losing end. But he can be bribed. Offer a filet mignon (or even a French fry), and he'll show you all sorts of tricks you never knew he'd learned. He's also a gifted mischief maker, and you can be sure he's working on a plan to get into your refrigerator. But even if he gets caught, he knows you won't be able to stay mad at him for long.

Turnabout is fair play, and a Frenchie Pug can't stay mad at people, either. Although he's mostly a one-family kind of dog, he pretty much gets along with everyone, and he's terrific as a child's companion. He makes a great apartment dog; in fact, he's better off avoiding too much strenuous activity and hot weather because he can overheat easily. And if you take him swimming to cool off, make sure the water's not over his head—Frenchie Pugs are known to have the buoyancy of cinder blocks.

Many Frenchie Pugs snuffle and snore (light sleepers, take note!), and they're a little heavy to be considered lapdogs. But there's something so endearing about a Frenchie Pug snoozing on your lap that you're certain not to mind a few sniffles or snorts. They weigh from 15 to 30 pounds (7–14 kg) and are most frequently seen in black, brindle, cream, or fawn, either solid or on a white background. Those short stiff hairs can weave their way into upholstery (and yes, he will be lounging about on your furniture), so frequent brushing, which only takes a minute, is advisable.

activeness	●●●●○
barking	●●●○○
dog friendliness	●●●●●
grooming	●●●●●
people friendliness	●●●●●
shedding	●●○○○
trainability	●●●●●

Cavapoo

Affable, eager, and a little impish, the Cavapoo is a cutie whose high-toned heritage belies her comic charm. And whether strutting it up in the city or sweetly swinging in a hammock, she's happiest when you're at her side.

Sugar and spice combine to make something very nice in the Cavapoo. The sugar comes from the super-sweet Cavalier King Charles Spaniel, and the spice from the more independent-minded Poodle. It's an immensely appealing combination.

On her spicy side, she insists on an action-packed lifestyle, frequently flouncing off to the park to gad about with her pals and orchestrate an escapade or two. And once she turns on that trickster twinkle in her eye, she's bound to get everyone around her in on the fun. Be it a high-speed chase or a round of "look-how-cute-I-am," this irresistible little dog demands full participation from her loved ones.

Now for her sugary side. The Cavapoo is just as endearing as she is exacting, and is known for her loving nature and uncanny ability to figure out just what it will take to make you crack a smile, whether it's a loving lick, an offered paw, or a full-blown comedy show. She loves to sit on laps, go for rides, and check out all the best outdoor cafes (especially if she can make friends along the way.)

But back to that spicy side. She'll expect a personal trainer (that's you) to keep her in shape with daily walks around the city, plus indoor workouts on rainy days (children may apply for the position of playmate, as may other dogs—she's not fussy about her friends). Oh, and she'll need a personal chef (you again) to create canine cuisine that thrills her palate (don't worry, she'll happily share your plate if you don't come up with something satisfactory).

Cavapoos can have either a Toy or Miniature Poodle parent. Those with a Toy parent weigh 6–12 pounds (3–5 kg), and those with a Miniature parent weigh 12–20 pounds (5–9 kg). Almost any color is possible, but red, black, and gold, either solid or patched, are most prevalent. Coat types can vary from a mixture of wavy and curly to flat, straight hair, with the curlier hair tending to be non-shedding and the straighter hair shedding more, though not excessively. Either way, she'll need a hairstylist to brush her at least every other day to prevent bad hair days, and she'll expect you to take her to visit the doggy salon every month or two.

activeness	●●●●○
barking	●●○○○
dog friendliness	●●●●●
grooming	●●●●●
people friendliness	●●●●●
shedding	●●○○○
trainability	●●●●○

Labradoodle

This is one celebrity canine who doesn't read his own press—and with his rave reviews, he doesn't need to. Easygoing and self-assured, the Labradoodle is a modest mister who's just happy to hang out with his friends.

He's a self-made bloke, the Cary Grant of designer dogs. Born of working-class Labrador Retriever and Standard Poodle parents, his destiny seemed laid out ahead of him as a working dog. Though he was good at his job, his handsome looks and winning personality propelled him to greater fame, and soon he was on the A-list of every chic club in town.

The Labradoodle doesn't let celebrity go to his head, however. He's a gregarious fellow who doesn't judge people by their position. Actually, he's more interested in whether their car has four-wheel drive, so he can get where he wants to go. He's a nature lover, with a special interest in waterfowl, thanks to his outdoorsy parents.

This is a casual guy who won't mind sloshing through puddles without rain gear, and in fact prefers it. He'll think nothing of showing up with a bandanna around his neck and his hair still wet from a swim. But he cleans up so well, he can easily switch from a down-home kerchief at the beach to a diamond-studded collar at dinner.

He likes his sports, and is happy hobnobbing at the polo grounds (or just lounging on the sofa watching NASCAR). But he'd rather participate than watch, and his idea of paradise is a day at the beach chasing a ball, catching a curl, or snoozing in the shade, beach-bum style.

Despite his full social calendar, he always seems able to squeeze in one more playdate, especially with his favorite partners—kids. And you'll need to make sure he gets plenty of exercise every day. Labradoodles don't tire easily, and unless he's truly tuckered out, he can become creative in ways you don't really want to find out about.

Labradoodles can be Standard (50–65 pounds/ 23–30 kg), Medium (30–45 pounds/13–20 kg), or Miniature (15–25 pounds/7–12 kg). Color choices include cream, apricot (pages 92–93), red, blue, chocolate, and black, in silky fleece, spiraling wool, or hair coats. The non-shedding fleece and wool must be brushed several times a week, while the hair coat, which does shed, requires less grooming.

activeness	●●●●○
barking	●●●●○
dog friendliness	●●●○○
grooming	●●●●○
people friendliness	●●●●●
shedding	●●○○○
trainability	●●●○○

Yochon

This comely lad stops traffic wherever he goes. With a shake of his deliberately shaggy mane and a yappy "Yo!", the Yochon lets you know he's cool. But the hipper-than-thou attitude is mostly a put-on—he's really a good-natured guy.

Cute, capricious, and oh-so-cosmopolitan, the Yochon springs from the combination of the Bichon Frise and the Yorkshire Terrier. Nobody can quite agree on a label for this pup—Yochon, Bichon Yorkie, and Yorchon are all used with equal frequency—but everyone can agree this is an especially appealing guy, in looks and personality.

The typical Yochon combines the vigor and devotion of the Bichon with the devil-may-care doggedness of the Yorkie. The result is an ersatz tiny terror who's all bark and no bite, full of nerve and verve and ready to roll with whatever you have.

He'a a metrosexual mongrel who's happy to spend a day at the salon (whether doggy or human), or accompany you for an afternoon of window shopping with a side trip to an uppity-puppy bakery. But he's no snob or sissy. He's also eager to get his feet wet in the nearest puddle or roll in the wet grass, and he's great going out for a pass or fetching a Frisbee—well, if it's small. (But don't dare condescend to him: he's pint-sized but pugnacious.)

Cheerful, playful, and willing to please, the Yochon loves to go adventuring, but is able to satisfy his exercise needs with indoor games. He's also a quick study and learns tricks readily. Now a bit of bad news: as with both parent breeds, house-training can be a daunting task, so be prepared.

Yochons weigh from 7 to 13 pounds (3–6 kg), so if your goal is to carry yours around in a doggy tote, aim for the smallest pup when choosing among a litter. Otherwise, a larger puppy is a better choice, often being hardier and easier to raise.

Given the limited palettes of both parents, one might expect a smaller selection of coat colors. But that doesn't seem to be the case. Yochons are available in lovely shades of cream, blue and tan, black and tan, sable, and black. Those fashionably mussed locks, which can be either wavy or curly, have to be groomed every couple of days, though, and look their best with a trip to the puppy salon at least every couple of months. (He never claimed that he wasn't high maintenance!)

Jackabee

Wind him up and watch him go! The Jackabee is an around-the-clock mover and shaker, and he'll make sure you're in motion along with him. Load him up for a road trip, or run him 'round the rec room. It's always a merry marathon.

If Jackabees ran the world, a three-minute egg would take one minute, roads would have no speed limits, and humans would never sleep. And when a Jackabee moves into your home, everything is expected to happen on Jackabee time. Industrious, mischievous, and clever, Jackabees know how to squeeze two days into one.

A cross between the similarly rest-challenged Jack Russell Terrier and the follow-your-nose-wherever-it-goes Beagle, a Jackabee could hardly be expected to sit quietly and watch life go by. He has to be right in the middle of things, bouncing and barking. He's a canine kid at heart; that's probably why he loves kids, and why they love him.

Some call him a genius (some an evil genius), and it's easy to see why. He's brainy and inquisitive, with a knack for figuring things out. Whether it's sliding a stool over to the kitchen counter so he can jump up for some counter surfing, or scheming a way to open the gate so he can visit that hot little dog down the street, he's bound to work it out.

This fellow may be too wired to settle into apartment life, unless you're prepared to devote yourself to his full-time entertainment. He thrives on challenging physical and mental exercise, and he needs it every day. Otherwise he might—no, he will—wreak havoc on your home in his quest for stimulation. But if you have the time, few dogs are as much fun as a Jackabee. He can run, jump, run, catch, run, bark, and run some more for hours. He also enjoys swimming, digging, and hunting.

He's as affectionate and effusive as he is lively, ready to leap into a lap or lick a face. And thankfully, even a Jackabee has to sleep, and when he does, he loves to kick back with his special person and snuggle happily for hours.

Jackabees weigh about 15–30 pounds (7–14 kg). Most are white with patches of color, usually black, brown, or tan, or maybe a combination. Their coats can be short like a Beagle's, or longer, with a coarse, straight texture, depending on whether the Jack Russell parent has a short or wiry coat.

activeness	●●●●○
barking	●●●●○
dog friendliness	●●●●●
grooming	●●●●●
people friendliness	●●●●●
shedding	●●●○○
trainability	●●●●○

Zuchon

With her unabashed wild streak and laissez-faire locks, the Zuchon can't resist spreading her zeal for life to those around her. And though she'd rather be scheming than promenading, this high-spirited pup wows all she meets.

For the zany Zuchon (also known as the Shichon), life's nothing short of a comedy. With her bubbly Bichon Frise demeanor and playful Shih Tzu prowess, this mop-headed marvel transforms every half-hour play session into a hit sitcom—with you providing the laugh track, of course.

Though she's cuddly, perky, and loving, the Zuchon won't hesitate to remind you of her superstar status. She expects to have a full house at all her performances, topped off with a standing ovation after each encore. This animated pooch knows that she's adored by all, though she counts on her entourage (you) to keep her company in the limelight; she wants to save her best antics for her most devoted fans. After all, who better to test her new material on than her friends?

This little comedienne does like to get out, though, and she'll tolerate being driven around in her limo or toted about in a doggy purse, but she won't like being cooped up for long. The Zuchon has cameos to make, and besides, she needs her exercise.

She's a high-rise kind of dog, and enjoys the city life, though when she's away from the puparazzi, she will finally relax with her family. She likes to play games, is a quick study, and enjoys showing off the many tricks she's learned (in preparation for her career on the silver screen). And she especially enjoys snuggling up against silky pajamas and watching DVDs (preferably of her own stand-up routines). She's a light sleeper, and she's always ready to sound the alarm should there be bumps in the night. Somebody has to keep out the riffraff.

The Zuchon won't be too effective against intruders on her own. But that's your job, as is protecting her from being stepped on by oafish humans or hurt by larger dogs she may have accidentally insulted.

At only 12 to 14 pounds (5–6 kg), Zuchons are small but stylish. Their silky coats come in all the colors of the Shih Tzu rainbow, most often cream, sable, gray, tan, or black, either solid or patched. They should be brushed every day or two to maintain their good looks, and may need an occasional trim.

activeness	●●●●○
barking	●●●●○
dog friendliness	●●●○○
grooming	●●●●●
people friendliness	●●●●○
shedding	●●●○○
trainability	●●●○○

Malshi

This wee scholar's always got his nose in a book—except when he's sniffing out some A+ shenanigans. But he's no class clown: the Malshi would make a dapper date to a black-tie party, or a happy tagalong to the haberdasher.

The combination of two fun-loving though regal parents, the Maltese and the Shih Tzu, the Malshi is known for both his jaunty jesting and his dignified erudition. But don't be fooled by his studious airs and his pet precocity: he's reading up on ways to conquer the world. With a toss of his miniature mane and a "pay-attention-to-me" yap, he'll have the masses eating out of his paw in no time.

Actually, this little prince is all about sharing. He'll share your food, your bed, your lap, your friends, and as many good times as you care to make him part of. A shopping spree? Totally. (Be sure to stop at the jewelry store for that little diamante dog bone he's been eyeing to dress up his collar.) A bite to eat with the guys? A chap's gotta stay trim, but count him in. (He'll have steak, by the way.) A trip to the dog park? Um, not top of the list (he's not into crowds), but what the heck! In truth, chasing a ball, barking at leaves, and running around being a dog are his secret pleasures. (Spritz him with a little eau de cologne afterward, or tuck him in your bag for a visit to the opera—presto, his loftiness is restored.)

This is a playful pixie who won't take to staying in the background. He likes to be the center of attention, especially if that involves fun and games. He's very clever and learns quickly, but has a tendency to let his mind wander, wondering what he may be missing elsewhere. He's a guy who needs to be on the go, and while he can enjoy watching the world pass by from inside a little dog carrier, he won't be happy staying there—not when the world so obviously needs his direction.

At home, the Malshi likes to oversee whatever you're doing. He's very affectionate, is an avid lap warmer, and a playful type who's a natural with children. He's quite at home in an apartment, as long as he gets his exercise in. He's even a vociferous (if not terribly intimidating) watchdog.

He weighs in at only 6 to 15 pounds (3–7 kg). Coming from two abundantly coated parents, the Malshi's silken coat is, of course, luxurious. But that teddy-bear look requires daily brushing to prevent matting, and needs clipping a few times a year.

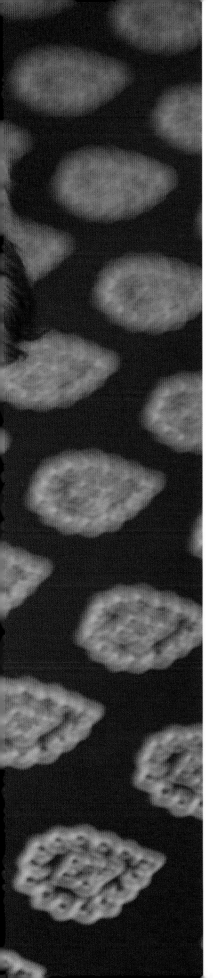

activeness	●●●●●
barking	●●●●○
dog friendliness	●●●○○
grooming	●●●○○
people friendliness	●●●○○
shedding	●●●○○
trainability	●●●●○

Maltipom

With a skip in her step and a glimmer in her eyes, the Maltipom is bound to enthrall. Though known for her fashionista flair, this sweetie's not too precious for some good ol' dogging around, be it digging a hole or dallying with kids.

With petit parents like the Pomeranian and the Maltese, the Maltipom could hardly help but be bijou-sized, only with the sparkle of a star. She's flirty and coy like her toy parents, and she can be a little naughty, but she knows how to get what she wants and she's not afraid to go for it. And if she goes too far, she knows that with a wag of her tail and a few well-placed kisses, all will be forgiven.

Just because she looks like a living doll doesn't mean you have to treat her like one. Sure, you can dress her up fancy and spend lots of time grooming her, but don't be surprised when she rolls her new outfit in the mud. She likes to get outside and bark and dig just like the real dog she is.

This pup is the one friend you can never say no to, and she seems born with that knowledge. A lap of your latte? A visit to the bowwow boutique? A ride in the country? How can you say no? Even at home, she's full of ideas. She loves a challenging game, whether it's learning some new trick or just getting a chance to roll around on the floor. Kids are

playmates of preference (as long as they're careful not to squish her). And when she's not in the thick of things, she doesn't mind playing cheerleader, barking encouragement to her favorites.

The Maltipom is an active little tyke, not one to sit around and wait for an invitation. She likes to go new places and try new things, and doesn't mind getting her hair mussed in the process. Despite her energy, she is very small, so she can't walk everywhere. But don't bother calling out the town car for her, she's happy to ride in a convertible, or in the doggy purse, so she can enjoy the fresh air.

She works well in leadership roles, and doesn't tolerate fools gladly. As astute as she is adorable, give her a chance to show off, and you'll be dazzled by her remarkable repertoire.

At only 8 to 14 pounds (4–6 kg), she is a special handful. You can fashion her straight hair—available in cream, sable, silver, white, and black and tan—in several styles. Just be sure to consult her first!

activeness	●●●●●
barking	●●●●●
dog friendliness	●●●○○
grooming	●●●○○
people friendliness	●●●●○
shedding	●●○○○
trainability	●●●●●

Jackapoo

This intrepid sidekick loves to go, go, go. He can't wait to feel the wind tickling his ears and see all the grand sights up close. It'd be no shocker if he wanted to drive—the Jackapoo knows all the shortcuts to mischief. Hang on tight!

The Jackapoo is a stuntman who's on an endless quest to push past new limits, the Captain Danger of the designer-dog world. What else would you expect from a cross between a daredevil Jack Russell Terrier and a perspicacious Poodle?

He's an equal-opportunity explorer, as excited by spelunking through the kitchen cabinets as he is by chasing a rabbit down a hole, as eager to push his way through the clothes closet as he is to forge through a rainforest, as ready to dig around under the sofa cushions as to launch an archaeological expedition for bones in the backyard. He's obviously not content to stay inside and watch the world go by—he's a player. And if he's not in trouble yet, stick around a few minutes.

The Jackapoo's style is jaunty, even rakish, but he's more concerned with function than fashion. Nonetheless, his good looks are effortless, and he can't help but turn heads whether he's in the city or the wilds. When it comes to getting places, the faster the better.

For all his nervy self-assurance, he's a dog with inner conflicts. How to merge his Jack Russell vivacity with his Poodley politeness? He tries, really he does, and when there's nothing to distract him, this pup's ahead of the curve when it comes to tackling even the toughest tricks.

Forget sleeping late. Or turning in early. He's the canine equivalent of caffeine, and you'll be out for a morning jog before the sun's cleared the horizon. Got kids? Great. Jackapoos love children's liveliness, and they can play tag or ball, and will generally make mayhem for hours. Oh, and forget peace and quiet—Jackapoos tend to be enamored of the sounds of their own voices.

In terms of looks, they're a hodgepodge, and may have short or long legs and a coat that's wiry, curly, wavy, broken, or short. They come in a variety of sizes, but most Jackapoos with a Miniature Poodle parent weigh in at 10 to 18 pounds (5–8 kg). The wiry or broken coats require brushing once a week; the wavy coat needs brushing every other day.

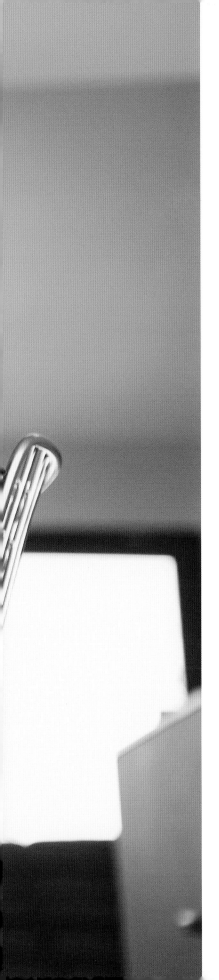

activeness	●●○○○
barking	●●○○○
dog friendliness	●●●○○
grooming	●●●●●
people friendliness	●●○○○
shedding	●●○○○
trainability	●●○○○

Pekeapoo

For this uptown girl, a stroll down the block is more like a strut down a runway, camera flashes and admiring gasps included. Though always à la mode, the Pekeapoo amplifies her striking looks with her one-of-a-kind personality.

Indulge yourself. If you have a taste for decadence, you need a designer dog with tastes to match—the persnickety Pekeapoo. A blend of the pampered Pekingese and perky Poodle, the Pekeapoo tends to be more Peke-ish than Poo-ish, and is never shy about reminding you of her royal roots.

She's a classic: dignified, self-assured, independent, and impressed with herself, deigning to give her approval only to her family and other select minions. And even though her circumstances may force her to fraternize with the masses, she holds her head high. She does her best, really, to cavort with other dogs at the dog park, but she does have her limits. After all, who knows where they have been?

Even you, her loyal servant, are not immune from her critical eye. After all, didn't you once try to feed her a can of grocery-store dog food? What were you thinking? Fortunately, all it takes is a few steaks, massages, car rides, trips to the park, high-fashion collars, designer beds, and endless fawning, and all is forgiven. She's just that kind of girl.

You wouldn't expect royalty to do your bidding or follow your orders, so don't be surprised when your commands are received as bizarre jokes. But there's a secret—if you make it worth her while, she doesn't mind showing off her I.Q. In fact, she can do a surprising number of downright doggish things. She cavorts and yaps and rolls and runs, especially if there's a child doing it alongside her, so she can justify her behavior if she gets caught.

The Pekeapoo likes to put in an appearance in front of her subjects daily, but she also doesn't mind being carried aloft rather than walking everywhere. She does like to get in some exercise every day, but she's definitely not into jogging, and she prefers promenading through the garden to backpacking in the woods. And with her hectic schedule, she needs her beauty sleep—on a satin pillow, of course.

She weighs from 7 to 20 pounds (3–9 kg), and her soft and cottony coat comes in black, tan, sable, gray, among others, either solid or spotted. As you might expect, this princess requires daily brushing.

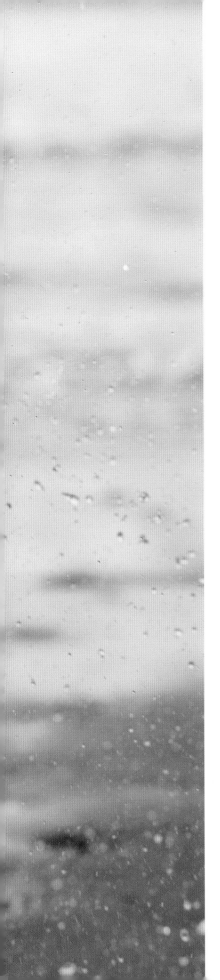

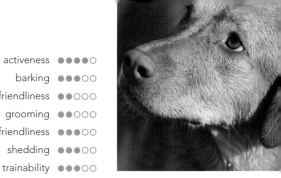

activeness	●●●●○
barking	●●●○○
dog friendliness	●●○○○
grooming	●●○○○
people friendliness	●●●○○
shedding	●●●○○
trainability	●●●○○

Chesador

Attaboy—shake it out! This sportsman loves a good dousing, be it from splashing along in the surf or dog-paddling around the lake. If you share the Chesador's enthusiasm for all things active, you'll get along swimmingly.

There's nothing like the smell of sea spray in the morning—at least, not for a Chesador. He's an outdoorsman, the offspring of generations of hunters, on both his Labrador and Chesapeake Bay Retriever sides. So he's the type who likes to get outside early, feel the frost on his toes, see his breath in the air, and plow into ice-crusted water for a morning dip before starting the day's duties.

This nature boy isn't just about enjoying the beauties of the wilderness. He's a hunter, never happier than if he has something to retrieve, preferably a downed duck or goose. But he'll settle for a ball, a stick, or pretty much anything that flies or floats. You may want to get one of those automatic ball throwers. Or hire some kids with strong arms. Oh, and a swimming pool would be nice if you don't have a place near the ocean.

He's a dog of simple needs. His dream house? A bungalow on the beach. Dream job? Hunting guide. Dream ride? An all-terrain truck on land, a powerboat by sea—although his own paws

are really his first choice, both for running and swimming. He loves to go hiking and trekking; coop him up, and he'll be one unhappy camper.

When it comes to common sense and survival skills, the Chesador is in top form. But he's never been much for rote learning, and he scoffs at trite tricks. Even so, he'll need to learn manners if he's to associate with civilized folks, and after a bout of charm school he can be downright gentlemanly. In fact, he's been known to roll over, play dead, and bark on command if the price is right (usually some beef jerky and the promise of a walk).

He can be a tough character, though, and he's not always happy inviting other dogs to join in his fun. He may take a few minutes to check out strangers, even kids, but once accepted, they're partners.

The Chesador is a stocky 55 to 80 pounds (25–36 kg). His short wash-and-wear coat comes in yellow, brown, and black, and luckily he isn't fussy about its care and is happiest when it's wet.

activeness	●●●○○
barking	●●○○○
dog friendliness	●●●●●
grooming	●●●●○
people friendliness	●●●●●
shedding	●●●○○
trainability	●●●●○

Cockalier

Ardent and adorable, the Cockalier delights all with her pure affection and gentle exuberance. As loyal as she is lovely, she's a constant companion, happy to accompany you on a hike up the hill or a jaunt to the jeweler's.

The Cockalier—also known as the King Cocker—is among dogdom's most fun-loving, caring creations. She's a love sponge that soaks it up, but gives it back with dividends. The daughter of the devoted Cavalier King Charles Spaniel and the congenial Cocker Spaniel (both of whom have been bred for generations for companionship), her goal in life would seem to be to kiss her way into your heart.

When it comes to love, she's the quintessential inamorata. She turns heads when she prances into a party, and proceeds to work the room like a true social butterfly. Never snooty, she greets everyone she sees with the same enthusiasm, whether dog, human, or even feline. All she asks is for her love to be returned. Oh, well, and maybe a good meal. And a tummy tickle or two—but she's so soft and cuddly, you'll be the one who can't get enough!

She's a lively girl, always ready to do a trick or play games with people of every age. With only a few lessons, she can beg, dance, roll over, and more. Popular, pretty, and intelligent—she's got it all.

The Cockalier is willing to learn and eager to please. Not that she has to worry: even when she slips up, she's too cute to get in trouble. And if she ever did, she could just hide in a pile of toy animals and never be picked out—the perfect camouflage!

She's a girl who's at home in the city, strolling the streets and contentedly letting others pet and dote on her, and she looks equally at home checking out a flea market as checking into the Ritz. But for all her city savvy, she just may surprise you when she gets a taste of the country. She takes right to the outdoor life, hunting and hiking with the best of them—even skinny-dipping.

Though she's sure of herself and aware of her appeal, a Cockalier is hardly a weight-watcher. She's proud of her chubby cheeks, and at 15 to 30 pounds (7–14 kg), she figures that just means there's more of her to love. Her soft wavy hair comes in spotted and solid patterns, in black, black and tan, red, and buff. It requires brushing every other day to keep her looking her best.

activeness	●●●●●
barking	●●●○○
dog friendliness	●●●○○
grooming	●●●●●
people friendliness	●●●○○
shedding	●○○○○
trainability	●●●○○

Maltapoo

They called it puppy love and, boy, were they right: this little lady melts hearts with her cuddly cunning and sweet je ne sais quoi. But the hype hasn't gone to her head. Always discerning, the Maltapoo knows when she's got it good.

The Maltapoo—or Maltipoo or Maltepoo, no one seems quite able to settle on a spelling—has been called the jewel of designer dogs. And that's a fitting title since this puppy comes from a marriage made between two of the first families of the dog world, the Maltese and the Poodles.

Her style is classic and her tastes are simple: only the best will do. She may turn her tiny nose up at a lesser cut of meat, or brush off a new acquaintance who's sucking up just to be seen with celebrity. She insists on the genuine article. That's one reason she's a little slow to warm up to new people; they have to prove themselves worthy before she bestows her endorsement upon them.

She's also slow to warm up to other dogs—no licking or touching please, or she may need another bath! But she will accept a few dogs, and humans too (especially young ones), into her circle of friends. And once you're in her circle, you're hers for good, and she'll let her inner puppy out to play and act like the silly dog she secretly longs to be.

She's an active girl, aware of her appearance and finicky about her physique. She can get some aerobic conditioning running from one end of the penthouse to the other, but what good is a trim figure unless others can admire it? She insists on getting out and about on a regular basis. In foul weather, if you can't carry her in a designer dog purse, she'll be more than happy to trot under your umbrella—as long as it matches her collar, that is.

But she's not only about going out in public dressed to the nines. At home she likes to snuggle and nestle deep into her goose-down bed, and she'll also contentedly recline alongside you as you read a book. (Of course, she'll insist you read aloud; this puppy will want in on the story, too.)

Maltapoos tend to be petite, weighing in at only 4 to 20 pounds (2–9 kg). Their long fur coats have a soft wave or can be curly, and are most often white, but also are seen in apricot, cream, black, gray, and spotted. Though low shedding, their fur tends to tangle easily, so they need to be brushed daily.

activeness	●●●●●
barking	●●●●●
dog friendliness	●●○○○
grooming	●●○○○
people friendliness	●●●○○
shedding	●●○○○
trainability	●●●●○

Jack Chi

All saunter and swagger, the Jack Chi acts like he's the biggest deal on the block. But despite his bold braggadocio and bad-boy image, he's a trickster and a charmer. And though he's happy to be scrappy, he also craves a cuddle.

All Jacked Up and Someplace to Go—that's this guy's motto. Known by some fans as a Jackhuahua, he's the rock star of designer dogs, with an outlaw attitude and a go-go lifestyle. The son of hipsters, the Jack Russell and the Chihuahua, he ended up besting them both and reinventing cool.

He's a dog that makes every scene and parties hard. He struts his stuff when all eyes are on him, and he's got no problem putting on a show. He has his own sense of style, and he does pretty much whatever he feels like. Rules don't apply to him.

That can make living with a Jack Chi a challenge, unless you keep him on a tight leash. He doesn't believe in curfews and sees nothing wrong with trashing the hotel room (also known as your home). But even hard-core nonconformists can be brought around to thinking your way, if there's something in it for them. As long as he gets to work out his pent-up energy, he'll respect your boundaries. He's also a natural-born performer, and if there's a chance to show off tricks, he'll be begging to learn more.

Being a top dog means staying in shape, and he likes to keep his body fit, even if it means indoor exercise. Have steps? He'll run up and down them a few thousand times. No steps? He can just run in a circle for a few miles. (You might be better off taking him out for a long prowl around the city.)

The Jack Chi has an image to uphold, and he won't back down from a challenge—even if it's from a big dog. They don't scare him. But, really, they ought to; he is a little guy, after all, and all the workouts in the world won't even the score there.

Beneath his bravado, the Jack Chi has a secret that more than makes up for his shortcomings: he's also a mellow family guy who loves to hang out with the kids, play games, and even do tricks. And when he finally passes out, he'd prefer to be in your arms.

Jack Chis weigh from 8 to 16 pounds (4–7 kg), and may be short- or long-legged. They generally have a wiry or smooth coat that tends to be some combination of white with tan or dark patches.

activeness	●●●●○
barking	●●●●○
dog friendliness	●●●●●
grooming	●●●●●
people friendliness	●●●●●
shedding	●●○○○
trainability	●●●●○

Schnoodle

Flashy and feisty, the Schnoodle is in the running for world's fastest fuzzy friend—in the dash for your affections, that is. But his finesse doesn't stop at the physical: this quick-witted buddy goes long in the quest for a good time.

Play ball, anyone? If you're looking for a partner, the Schnoodle has got you covered. A cross between a Schnauzer and a Poodle, he's been a part of the country-club set for thirty years, and is a classic in the designer-dog world. But he's not a dog who's satisfied with the status quo, so he's always looking for help in improving his game.

He was a jock before sports stars earned millions, and he's still in it for the love of the game. Track and field, swimming, and pretty much anything involving spheres—he's a star. (He does draw the line at polo, however, preferring to sit in the stands and rub shoulders with the beautiful people. Besides, he knows that the gorgeous dog in the bleachers gets all the attention. He isn't stupid.)

His Schnoodle smarts are one reason he's always on top of his game. He's a quick study, and knows every trick of the trade, including "sit," "speak," "beg," and "roll over." Not to mention a few plays of his own design, like raiding the fridge while you go see what he was barking at in the other room.

Life with a sports star isn't all glamour. You're going to have to do your part as personal trainer and manager. He'll need you to get out and do drills with him daily, running wind sprints or jogging, plus there's always ball practice, along with isometric exercises (in the form of long tugging sessions).

A Schnoodle appeals to active people who enjoy a mischievous sense of humor and a go-getting approach to life. But the joke will be on you if you don't keep up with him, because a bored Schnoodle can make mischief in ways you may not appreciate. They're super-alert and don't hesitate to bark at anything amiss—and some have a liberal definition of "amiss" and may bark at anything.

This versatile player comes in three sizes: Toy (under 10 pounds/5 kg), Miniature (10–20 pounds/ 5–9 kg), and Standard (20–50 pounds/9–23 kg). He's mostly seen in black, white, or apricot, and usually sports longer hair that varies between the harsh coat of the Schnauzer and the soft coat of the Poodle, and should be brushed every other day.

activeness	●●●●○
barking	●●●○○
dog friendliness	●●●●●
grooming	●○○○○
people friendliness	●●●●○
shedding	●●●●○
trainability	●●○○○

Puggle

What is it about the Puggle that makes him so popular? For starters, there's the friendliness factor. Oh, and that hyperkinetic tail. His puckish personality and soulful stare has made him the canine idol of the hybrid world.

Wrinkled face, stout body, short legs—not exactly what you'd expect of a superstar, unless you're talking about a Puggle, designer darling of the Hollywood haut monde. Maybe it's his farcical face, his attaboy attitude, or just his sheer animal magnetism—whatever the cause, wherever he goes, the Puggle earns the sort of adulation usually reserved for rock singers and movie stars.

With a tail that just keeps wagging, he's the proverbial cockeyed optimist. Why shouldn't he be, when a tilt of that rounded head or a blink of those expressive eyes has people rushing to fulfill his every whim? For a Puggle, life is good. He can sleep on the bed, munch on a bone, play with some toys, snuggle on a lap, and head out for a stroll around the block, where he'll be swamped with "oohs" and "ahhs" from adoring passersby. If he's really lucky, he'll run loose, find a scent, and immerse himself in the thrill of the hunt, oblivious to the frantic calls of his special person. (Absence makes the heart grow fonder, so by the time he finds you, he should be really fond.)

Part Beagle, part Pug, he just can't help but be his own dog. With neither parent known for trainability, you can't blame the Puggle for being true to his genes and thinking up novel ways to misunderstand you. He's afflicted by selective deafness—unable to hear you call from across the room, yet attuned to the faintest sound of the refrigerator door opening.

Clownish and affectionate, the Puggle makes a good playmate for active people and children. But though he has an easier time breathing than his scrunch-faced Pug parent, his snout is still pretty short (as are his legs), so he may not be the best jogging companion and could overheat easily.

They're slightly smaller than Beagles, weighing 15 to 30 pounds (7–14 kg), and are seen in Pug colors: fawn, silver, and black, usually with a black muzzle, occasionally with white or with a brown body and black saddle. Their coats are short, thick, and coarse, and require brushing to prevent excess shedding on your lap—which is where he likes to be, practicing the patented Puggle snuggle.

activeness	●●●●○
barking	●●●●○
dog friendliness	●●●○○
grooming	●●●●●
people friendliness	●●●●○
shedding	●●●○○
trainability	●●●○○

Silkchon

Shaggy but sophisticated, this gent takes the whole world in stride. Whether sweetly snoozing on a bead-tasseled pillow, effortlessly absorbing new tricks, or wildly chasing a rogue rodent, the handsome Silkchon makes life look easy.

The suave and satiny Silkchon saunters through life, oozing the charm and savoir faire of a dog who's got it all. The favored son of a bubbly Bichon Frise and a sassy Silky Terrier, he combines traits of each to make him the top cat of the dog world.

He's a smooth mover in whatever he pursues, and he easily manages to convince you that you want what he wants. A small nudge of the muzzle, a touch of the paw, and he practically hypnotizes you to do his bidding. Feed him, pet him, buy him new toys—and that's just the beginning of his demands. How about a velvet bed, silver inlaid harness, and personal dog walker? (Who says he's spoiled?)

Actually, forget the dog walker. He wants you to be the one alongside him, day or night. Of course, his idea of nightlife is barking at things that go thump, and his terrier roots can pull him past the bright lights and into the hinterlands. He may look citified, but he's definitely got an unfettered side. He doesn't mind digging in the dirt when the chance arises, either. (Oh, relax—it'll wash off.)

His love of the chase extends to squirrels (and sometimes cats), but as long as he's inside he can control his wild impulses and live quite peaceably. (Well, with cats. Not squirrels. He has his pride.) As for people, he likes to act a little aloof when he first meets strangers, but once they pass his litmus test, he's ready to accept them as new best friends. Children automatically pass the test.

He's a playboy, and he loves playing ball, tag, and "look-at-how-smart-I-am!" He can pick up tricks in an instant, but he sometimes seems to think he's too cool to actually perform them. But for all his cute cunning, the best is the way he makes you feel how special he thinks you are. You're never alone with a Silkchon at your side, whether ambling down the street or falling asleep in front of the fireplace.

Silkchons weigh about 10 to 16 pounds (5–7 kg). As you might expect, their coats are, in fact, silky, and long. They come in most solid colors, as well as in sable, and need to be groomed every other day. An occasional clip helps keep them in trim.

activeness	●●●●○
barking	●●●●●
dog friendliness	●●●●○
grooming	●●●●●
people friendliness	●●●○○
shedding	●●●○○
trainability	●●●○○

Yorktese

Teeny but not timid, small but with gall—any way you say it, the Yorktese's personality far exceeds her slight size. While her wily ways can get her into a tight squeeze or two, don't worry: pulling a Houdini is all part of the show.

It makes perfect sense that this little firecracker would have a combustible personality. With a tiny but tumultuous Yorkshire Terrier as one parent and a mite-sized but mighty Maltese as the other, she was bound to be one small package of dynamite.

Everything she does, she does with fire. She won't merely walk into a room, she'll explode into it. She doesn't simply greet a new friend, she blitzes them with a chrysanthemum of kisses. Her fiery persona also makes her take chances she probably shouldn't. She'll bark at big dogs; she'll chase the cat (who is often larger than she is); and she won't back down from a challenge. But then, she knows you'll be there to pull her out of any scrapes.

Not surprisingly, this sparky sprout can be a terror to train. She can pack more obstinacy into her few pounds than most dogs thrice her size would manage, and she'll stick her nose up in the air if you try to bribe her with mere dog treats. (Just who do you think you're dealing with?) But once you've found the right bonbons, she's a dazzling trickster.

Yes, she's been accused of having an attitude, but come on—one look at that baby-doll face and who could honestly blame her? She's the cutest kid on the block, and she has every intention of taking advantage of the situation. But she's also as sweet as she is sightly, and she loves to play all sorts of games with you and the other kids in the family—as long as they remember she is delicate.

She likes to run and bark and let everyone know exactly what she thinks at all times. Fortunately, at only 5 to 10 pounds (2–5 kg), she can get a lot of exercise inside an apartment. But she still needs to get out in the world, either on foot or in a doggy purse. After all, how else will everyone know whether they're doing things correctly?

Her silky hair sometimes sprouts in a variety of directions, giving her a rakish bedhead look. But with age, it can grow long and alluring. It requires gentle brushing every couple of days, and comes in a variety of patterns and colors, including black and tan, cream, black, red, and white.

activeness	●●●●○
barking	●●○○○
dog friendliness	●●●○○
grooming	●●●●○
people friendliness	●●●●○
shedding	●●○○○
trainability	●●●●○

Whoodle

Wild and wacky, the Whoodle has a cultivated knack for tomfoolery. But he's no joker: whether gamboling about the yard or sneaking a doggy treat, he's a paws-on pup who'll want in on all the action—hugs and snuggles included.

The Whoodle is a gambler at heart, a daring dog willing to take on the odds. He's got an ace up his sleeve—his unique combination of Poodle smarts and Soft-Coated Wheaten Terrier intrigue.

Crafty, slick, and a bit of a rogue, a Whoodle can wheedle his way into whatever game presents itself. He's a lady's man who knows how to turn on the charm to get what he wants—and how to make those big puppy-dog eyes get him out of all sorts of scrapes. But he's no love-'em-and-leave-'em cad. When he gives his love, he gives it all. And he's not shy about showing his feelings, as long as they're returned in kind. Public displays of affection can only add to his playboy image.

The Whoodle never fails to elicit attention from those who appreciate his worldly image. He takes the attention in stride, though, and even seems to thrive on it, doling out his favors like casino chips. Human, dog, cat—it makes little difference to him who the admirer is as long as they take care to show him the proper amount of respect.

Some call him a card, and it may be true, because he's definitely a joker. He has a waggish sense of humor and likes playing tricks almost as much as he likes playing games. Don't worry, he doesn't spend all his time at the tables (though he doesn't mind begging there a bit). He'll bet on anything. Can he catch that ball? Beat you to the door you accidentally left open? Snatch that steak off the counter without you noticing? (Making sure he loses some of the more audacious bets is the best way to cure his risk-taking behavior.)

With his high energy, he needs lots of physical exercise and mental training to control his urges to gambol inside the house. Given his druthers, he'd like to lounge around the pool (even if it's a kiddie pool) and take it easy. But while he does appreciate the finer things in life, he's used to highs and lows and can make do with whatever he's given.

He's handsome and solid, weighing between 25 and 50 pounds (11–23 kg), and wears his shaggy hair in solid cream, black, white, sable, or gray.

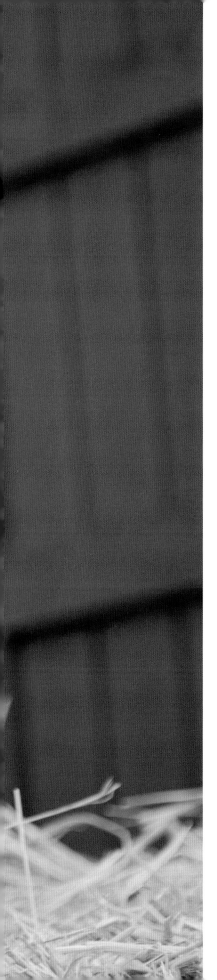

activeness	●●●●○
barking	●●●●○
dog friendliness	●●○○○
grooming	●○○○○
people friendliness	●●●○○
shedding	●●○○○
trainability	●●●○○

Brat

Keep Manhattan, Just Give Me That Countryside—that's the motto of this rustic rascal. Sharp, sturdy, and seriously playful, the Brat is like a favorite country cousin who's always ready to kick up a bit of mischief.

It's called "brattitude"—that brash approach a Brat adopts so freely with all around her. She is a combo of two blue-blood classics, the Boston Terrier and the American Rat Terrier, popularized by Teddy Roosevelt. But this child of old-money families makes her own way in the world, and would rather help park cars than stroll Park Avenue.

Her provincial ways may raise a few eyebrows in highbrow society, but she's a favorite with folks who like to get down and dirty with their dog. A Brat doesn't mind digging a few holes, rolling in some mud, or dishing some dirt. It's part of her tough-dog image. The truth is, though, it's all a show. The real Brat is more scamp than scoundrel.

Sure, she has a nose for trouble. That's why she also has those enormous pricked ears—so she can hear you coming and quickly plaster her patented "Who, me?" look all over her face, a trick she mastered as a precocious pup. It can't help but make you smile, even when she has the remnants of your missing wallet hanging out of her mouth.

Then there's also the Brat she doesn't want you to advertise—the Brat that loves to cuddle in mom's lap or help dad work on the truck. The one that has a soft spot for kids and would gladly share an ice-cream cone with one. And the one that can roll over, beg, speak, and play dead on command, and loves to show off. But all that's just bad for the image, so keep it quiet. She'd rather preserve her reputation as a holy hog-tying terror.

A word of advice: a bored Brat is a bad Brat. While she doesn't need hours of exercise, she needs lots of excitement, with games and outings. Just don't feel too left out when she steals all the attention.

A slenderized version of a Boston Terrier, the Brat has a strong square muzzle, super-sized ears, and a svelte torso. She weighs in at about 10–20 pounds (5–9 kg), and sports a short coat of soft shiny hair. Her favorite colors are brindle, black, black and tan, and seal brown, all either alone or with flashy white markings on the feet, face, and neck—her very own version of barnyard bling.

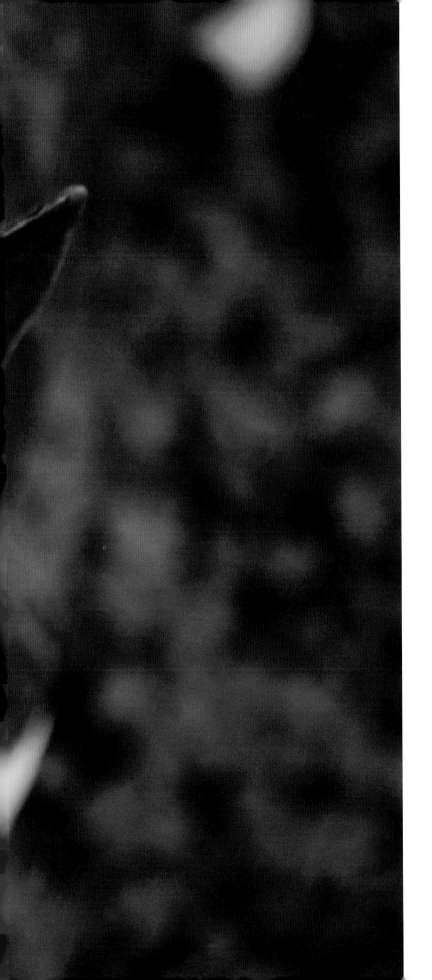

A Directory of Crossbreeds

While there are untold numbers of possible hybrid combinations, some crossbreeds have made a name for themselves. Here's a list of over 400 recognized designer-dog breeds—some common, some rare—along with their purebred parents.

CROSSBREED	PUREBRED PARENTS	
Affenpoo	Affenpinscher	x Poodle
Alusky	Alaskan Malamute	x Siberian Husky
American Bull Jack	American Bulldog	x Jack Russell Terrier
American Bullnese	French Bulldog	x Pekingese
American Eagle Dog	American Eskimo	x Beagle
American Gointer	English Pointer	x Golden Retriever
American Rat Pinscher	American Rat Terrier	x Min. Pinscher
Ausky	Australian Cattle Dog	x Siberian Husky
Aussiepoo	Australian Shepherd	x Poodle
Ausstzu	Min. Australian Shepherd	x Shih Tzu
Austipap	Min. Australian Shepherd	x Papillon
Australian Silky Terrier	Australian Terrier	x Silky Terrier
Bagle Hound	Basset Hound	x Beagle
Bashar	Basset Hound	x Chinese Sharpei
Baskimo	American Eskimo	x Basset Hound
Basschshund	Basset Hound	x Dachshund
Basset Retriever	Basset Hound	x Golden Retriever
Bassetoodle	Basset Hound	x Poodle
Basston	Basset Hound	x Boston Terrier
Bassugg	Basset Hound	x Pug
BD Terrier	American Bulldog	x Bull Terrier
Be Apso	Beagle	x Lhasa Apso
Bea Griffon	Beagle	x Brussels Griffon
Beabull	Beagle	x Bulldog
Beacol	Beagle	x Bearded Collie
Beagador	Beagle	x Labrador Retriever
Beagleman	Beagle	x Doberman Pinscher
Beaglier	Beagle	x Cavalier King Charles
Beaglolo	Beagle	x Bolognese
Beago	Beagle	x Golden Retriever
Beatzu	Beagle	x Shih Tzu
Bernefie	Bernese Mountain Dog	x Newfoundland
Bichomo	American Eskimo	x Bichon Frise
Bichon Yorkie	Bichon Frise	x Yorkshire Terrier
Bichonaranian	Bichon Frise	x Pomeranian
Biewer Yorkie	Biewer	x Yorkshire Terrier
Biton	Bichon Frise	x Coton de Tulear
Bocker	Beagle	x Cocker Spaniel
Bodach	Boston Terrier	x Dachshund

CROSSBREED	PUREBRED PARENTS	
Bodacion	Bearded Collie	x Dalmatian
Bogle	Beagle	x Boxer
Boglen Terrier	Beagle	x Boston Terrier
Bolo Tzu	Bolognese	x Shih Tzu
Bolonoodle	Bolognese	x Poodle
Bolosilk	Bolognese	x Silky Terrier
Borador	Border Collie	x Labrador Retriever
Bosapso	Boston Terrier	x Lhasa Apso
Boshih	Boston Terrier	x Shih Tzu
Boskimo	American Eskimo	x Boston Terrier
Bospin	Boston Terrier	x Min. Pinscher
Bossipoo	Boston Terrier	x Poodle
Bostchon	Bichon Frise	x Boston Terrier
Bostillon	Boston Terrier	x Papillon
Bostinese	Boston Terrier	x Pekingese
Boston Spaniel	Boston Terrier	x Cocker Spaniel
Bowzer	Basset Hound	x Min. Schnauzer
Brat	American Rat Terrier	x Boston Terrier
Broodle Griffon	Brussels Griffon	x Poodle
Brottweiler	Brussels Griffon	x Rottweiler
Brug	Brussels Griffon	x Pug
BT Walker	Boxer	x Treeing Walker
Bugg	Boston Terrier	x Pug
Bull Boxer	Boxer	x Bulldog
Bullmasador	Bullmastiff	x Labrador Retriever
Bullmatian	Bulldog	x Dalmatian
Bullpei	Bulldog	x Chinese Sharpei
Bully Basset	Basset Hound	x Bulldog
Bushland Terrier	Cairn Terrier	x Scottish Terrier
Cadoodle	Collie	x Poodle
Cairland Terrier	Cairn Terrier	x W. Highland White Terrier
Cairmal	Cairn Terrier	x Maltese
Cairnese	Cairn Terrier	x Havanese
Caretzu	Cairn Terrier	x Shih Tzu
Carkie	Cairn Terrier	x Yorkshire Terrier
Carnauzer	Cairn Terrier	x Min. Schnauzer
Cattle Collie Dog	Australian Cattle Dog	x Collie
Cavachin	Cavalier King Charles	x Japanese Chin
Cavachon	Bichon Frise	x Cavalier King Charles

Chug

Cockapoo

Chion

Doxiepoo

CROSSBREED	PUREBRED PARENTS	
Cavalon	Cavalier King Charles	x	Papillon
Cavamalt	Cavalier King Charles	x	Maltese
Cavamo	American Eskimo	x	Cavalier King Charles
Cavanese	Cavalier King Charles	x	Havanese
Cavapoo	Cavalier King Charles	x	Poodle
Cavaton	Cavalier King Charles	x	Coton de Tulear
Cavatzu	Cavalier King Charles	x	Shih Tzu
Cavestie	Cavalier King Charles	x	W. Highland White Terrier
Cavottish	Cavalier King Charles	x	Scottish Terrier
Cheeks	Chihuahua	x	Pekingese
Cherokee Monarch	Papillon	x	Russian Toy Terrier
Chesador	Chesapeake Bay Retriever	x	Labrador Retriever
Chi Apso	Chihuahua	x	Lhasa Apso
Chichi	Chihuahua	x	Chinese Crested
Chichon	Bichon Frise	x	Chihuahua
Chigi	Chihuahua	x	Corgi
Chimation	Chihuahua	x	Dalmatian
China Jack	Chinese Crested	x	Jack Russell Terrier
Chinaranian	Chinese Crested	x	Pomeranian
Chinese Frise	Bichon Frise	x	Chinese Crested
Chinocker	Cocker Spaniel	x	Japanese Chin
Chinwa	Chihuahua	x	Japanese Chin
Chion	Chihuahua	x	Papillon
Chipin	Chihuahua	x	Min. Pinscher
Chiranian	Chihuahua	x	Pomeranian
Chiweenie	Chihuahua	x	Dachshund
Chonzer	Bichon Frise	x	Min. Schnauzer
Chorkie	Chihuahua	x	Yorkshire Terrier
Chug	Chihuahua	x	Pug
Chussel	Brussels Griffon	x	Chihuahua
Cluminger Spaniel	Clumber Spaniel	x	English Springer
Cockachon	Bichon Frise	x	Cocker Spaniel
Cockalier	Cavalier King Charles	x	Cocker Spaniel

CROSSBREED	PUREBRED PARENTS	
Cockamo	American Eskimo	x	Cocker Spaniel
Cockapin	Cocker Spaniel	x	Min. Pinscher
Cockapoo	Cocker Spaniel	x	Poodle
Cockatzu	Cocker Spaniel	x	Shih Tzu
Cocker Pug	Cocker Spaniel	x	Pug
Cockeranian	Cocker Spaniel	x	Pomeranian
Cockerton	Cocker Spaniel	x	Coton de Tulear
Cockinese	Cocker Spaniel	x	Pekingese
Cogol	Cocker Spaniel	x	Golden Retriever
Cojack	Jack Russell Terrier	x	Pembroke Welsh Corgi
Colonial Cocker Spaniel	American Cocker Spaniel	x	English Cocker Spaniel
Comfort Retriever	Cocker Spaniel	x	Golden Retriever
Corkie	Cocker Spaniel	x	Yorkshire Terrier
Cosheltie	Collie	x	Shetland Sheepdog
Coton Beagle	Coton de Tulear	x	Beagle
Coton Tzu	Coton de Tulear	x	Shih Tzu
Cotonese	Coton de Tulear	x	Maltese
Cotralian	Cocker Spaniel	x	Min. Australian Shepherd
Crested Havanese	Chinese Crested	x	Havanese
Crested Malt	Chinese Crested	x	Maltese
Crested Schnauzer	Chinese Crested	x	Min. Schnauzer
Crustie	Chinese Crested	x	Yorkshire Terrier
Dameranian	Dachshund	x	Pomeranian
Daug	Dachshund	x	Pug
Dobsky	Doberman Pinscher	x	Old English Sheepdog
Doodle	Dachshund	x	Poodle
Doodleman Pinscher	Doberman Pinscher	x	Poodle
Dorgi	Dachshund	x	Pembroke Welsh Corgi
Dorkie	Dachshund	x	Yorkshire Terrier
Doxie Scot	Dachshund	x	Scottish Terrier
Doxiechon	Bichon Frise	x	Dachshund
Doxiepin	Dachshund	x	Min. Pinscher
Doxiepoo	Dachshund	x	Poodle

CROSSBREEDS	PUREBRED PARENTS	
Doxle	Beagle	x	Dachshund
Dualanese	Bolognese	x	Havanese
Engapoo	English Springer Spaniel	x	Poodle
English Boston Bull	Boston Terrier	x	Bulldog
English Bull Walker	Bulldog	x	Treeing Walker
English King Spaniel	Cavalier King Charles	x	English Toy Spaniel
English Mastweiler	Mastiff	x	Rottweiler
English Toy Cocker Spaniel	Cocker Spaniel	x	English Toy Spaniel
English Toy Griffon	Brussels Griffon	x	English Toy Spaniel
Eskifon	American Eskimo	x	Brussels Griffon
Eskijac	American Eskimo	x	Jack Russell Terrier
Eskland	American Eskimo	x	Shetland Sheepdog
Euro Mountain Sheparnese	Bernese Mountain Dog	x	German Shepherd
Ewokian	Havanese	x	Pomeranian
Faux Frenchbo Bulldog	Boston Terrier	x	French Bulldog
Fochon	Bichon Frise	x	Toy Fox Terrier
Foodle	Poodle	x	Toy Fox Terrier
Fotzu	Shih Tzu	x	Toy Fox Terrier
Fourche Terrier	W. Highland White Terrier	x	Yorkshire Terrier
Foxingese	Pekingese	x	Toy Fox Terrier
Foxker	Cocker Spaniel	x	Toy Fox Terrier
Foxton	Boston Terrier	x	Toy Fox Terrier
Foxy Rat Terrier	American Rat Terrier	x	Toy Fox Terrier
Foxy Russell	Jack Russell Terrier	x	Toy Fox Terrier
Frenchie Pug	French Bulldog	x	Pug
Frengle	Beagle	x	French Bulldog
Giant Schnoodle	Giant Schnauzer	x	Standard Poodle
Glechon	Beagle	x	Bichon Frise
Goberian	Golden Retriever	x	Siberian Husky
Golden Cocker	Cocker Spaniel	x	Golden Retriever
Golden Irish	Golden Retriever	x	Irish Setter

CROSSBREEDS	PUREBRED PARENTS	
Golden Labrador	Golden Retriever	x	Labrador Retriever
Golden Mountain Dog	Bernese Mountain Dog	x	Golden Retriever
Golden Pyrenees	Golden Retriever	x	Great Pyrenees
Goldendoodle	Golden Retriever	x	Poodle
Goldmaraner	Golden Retreiver	x	Weimaraner
Goldmation	Dalmatian	x	Golden Retriever
Gollie	Collie	x	Golden Retriever
Griffichon	Bichon Frise	x	Brussels Griffon
Griffonese	Brussels Griffon	x	Pekingese
Griffonland	Brussels Griffon	x	W. Highland White Terrier
Hava Apso	Havanese	x	Lhasa Apso
Hava Welsh	Havanese	x	Welsh Terrier
Hava Wheat	Havanese	x	Wheaten Terrier
Havachin	Havanese	x	Japanese Chin
Havachon	Bichon Frise	x	Havanese
Havamalt	Havanese	x	Maltese
Havanestie	Havanese	x	W. Highland White Terrier
Havapeke	Havanese	x	Pekingese
Havashire	Havanese	x	Yorkshire Terrier
Havashu	Havanese	x	Shih Tzu
Havaton	Coton de Tulear	x	Havanese
Highland Maltie	Maltese	x	W. Highland White Terrier
Imo Inu	American Eskimo	x	Shiba Inu
Irish Saint	Irish Terrier	x	Saint Bernard
Italian Bichon	Bichon Frise	x	Italian Greyhound
Jacairn	Cairn Terrier	x	Jack Russell Terrier
Jachon	Bichon Frise	x	Japanese Chin
Jack Chi	Chihuahua	x	Jack Russell Terrier
Jack Rat Terrier	American Rat Terrier	x	Jack Russell Terrier
Jackabee	Beagle	x	Jack Russell Terrier
Jackapoo	Jack Russell Terrier	x	Poodle

Goldendoodle

Goldendoodle

Goldendoodle Mini

Jack Chi

Labradoodle

Maltapoo

Oripei

CROSSBREED	PUREBRED PARENTS		
Jackhuahua	Chihuahua	x	Jack Russell Terrier
Jackie Bichon	Bichon Frise	x	Jack Russell Terrier
Jafox	Japanese Chin	x	Toy Fox Terrier
Jaland	Japanese Chin	x	W. Highland White Terrier
Japeke	Japanese Chin	x	Pekingese
Japillon	Japanese Chin	x	Papillon
Jarkie	Japanese Chin	x	Yorkshire Terrier
Jatese	Japanese Chin	x	Maltese
Jatzu	Japanese Chin	x	Shih Tzu
Kashon	Bichon Frise	x	Cairn Terrier
Kerrblushcnauz	Kerry Blue Terrier	x	Min. Schnauzer
Kerry Wheaten	Kerry Blue Terrier	x	Wheaten Terrier
Kimola	American Eskimo	x	Lhasa Apso
King Cavrin	Cavalier King Charles	x	Cairn Terrier
King Charles Yorkie	Cavalier King Charles	x	Yorkshire Terrier
King Cocker	Cavalier King Charles	x	Cocker Spaniel
King Schnauzer	Cavalier King Charles	x	Min. Schnauzer
La Pom	Lhasa Apso	x	Pomeranian
Lab'Aire	Airedale Terrier	x	Labrador Retriever
Labbe	Beagle	x	Labrador Retriever
Labmaraner	Labrador Retriever	x	Weimaraner
Lab Pointer	Labrador Retriever	x	English Pointer
Labradinger	English Toy Spaniel	x	Labrador Retriever
Labradoodle	Labrador Retriever	x	Poodle
Labralas	Labrador Retriever	x	Vizsla
Labrottie	Labrador Retriever	x	Rottweiler
Lachon	Bichon Frise	x	Lhasa Apso
Lhacocker	Cocker Spaniel	x	Lhasa Apso
Lhaffon	Brussels Griffon	x	Lhasa Apso
Lhasalier	Cavalier King Charles	x	Lhasa Apso
Lhasanese	Lhasa Apso	x	Pekingese
Lhasapoo	Lhasa Apso	x	Poodle
Lhatese	Lhasa Apso	x	Maltese

CROSSBREED	PUREBRED PARENTS		
Malchi	Chihuahua	x	Maltese
Malinois	Belgian Malinois	x	German Shepherd
Malkie	Maltese	x	Yorkshire Terrier
Malshi	Maltese	x	Shih Tzu
Maltapoo	Maltese	x	Poodle
Malteagle	Beagle	x	Maltese
Maltepoo	Maltese	x	Poodle
Maltichon	Bichon Frise	x	Maltese
Maltipin	Maltese	x	Min. Pinscher
Maltipom	Maltese	x	Pomeranian
Maltipoo	Maltese	x	Poodle
Malzer	Maltese	x	Min. Schnauzer
Mastador	Labrador Retriever	x	Mastiff
Mastibull	American Bulldog	x	Mastiff
Mauxie	Dachshund	x	Maltese
Mauzer	Maltese	x	Min. Schnauzer
Meagle	Beagle	x	Min. Pinscher
Min. Australian Shepterrier	Australian Terrier	x	Min. Australian Shepherd
Min. Bulldog	Bulldog	x	Pug
Min. English Bulldach	Bulldog	x	Dachshund
Min. Schnaupin	Min. Pinscher	x	Min. Schnauzer
Min. Schnauzzie	Min. Australian Shepherd	x	Min. Schnauzer
Min. Schnoxie	Dachshund	x	Min. Schnauzer
Miniboz	Boston Terrier	x	Min. Schnauzer
Minnie Jack	Jack Russell Terrier	x	Min. Pinscher
Morkie	Maltese	x	Yorkshire Terrier
Mountain Bulldog	Bernese Mountain Dog	x	Bulldog
Mountain Mastiff	Bernese Mountain Dog	x	Mastiff
Muggin	Min. Pinscher	x	Pug
Old Anglican Bulldogge	American Pit Bull Terrier	x	Bulldog
Olde Bulldog	American Bulldog	x	Bulldog
Oripei	Chinese Sharpei	x	Pug
Papastzu	Papillon	x	Shih Tzu

CROSSBREEDS	PUREBRED PARENTS		
Paperanian	Papillon	x	Pomeranian
Papichon	Bichon Frise	x	Papillon
Papipoo	Papillon	x	Poodle
Papitese	Maltese	x	Papillon
Papshund	Dachshund	x	Papillon
Patterbea	Beagle	x	Patterdale Terrier
Patton Terrier	Boston Terrier	x	Patterdale Terrier
Peagle	Beagle	x	Pekingese
Pekalier	Cavalier King Charles	x	Pekingese
Pekeachon	Bichon Frise	x	Pekingese
Pekeapap	Papillon	x	Pekingese
Pekeapin	Min. Pinscher	x	Pekingese
Pekeapoo	Pekingese	x	Poodle
Pekeatese	Maltese	x	Pekingese
Pekehund	Dachshund	x	Pekingese
Pineranian	Min. Pinscher	x	Pomeranian
Pinnypoo	Min. Pinscher	x	Poodle
Pom Terrier	Pomeranian	x	Toy Fox Terrier
Pomanauzer	Min. Schnauzer	x	Pomeranian
Pomapoo	Pomeranian	x	Poodle
Pomapug	Pomeranian	x	Pug
Pomcoton	Coton de Tulear	x	Pomeranian
Pomerat	American Rat Terrier	x	Pomeranian
Pomimo	American Eskimo	x	Pomeranian
Pominese	Pekingese	x	Pomeranian
Pomshi	Pomeranian	x	Shiba Inu
Pomsilk	Pomeranian	x	Silky Terrier
Pomston	Boston Terrier	x	Pomeranian
Poocan	Cairn Terrier	x	Poodle
Poochin	Japanese Chin	x	Poodle
Poochis	Chinese Crested	x	Poodle
Poochon	Bichon Frise	x	Poodle
Poogle	Beagle	x	Poodle
Pookimo	American Eskimo	x	Poodle
Poolky	Poodle	x	Silky Terrier
Pooshi	Poodle	x	Shiba Inu
Pootalian	Italian Greyhound	x	Poodle
Pooton	Coton de Tulear	x	Poodle
Poovanese	Havanese	x	Poodle
Poshies	Pomeranian	x	Shetland Sheepdog
Pugairn	Cairn Terrier	x	Pug
Pugapoo	Poodle	x	Pug
Pugese	Chinese Crested	x	Pug
Puggat	American Rat Terrier	x	Pug
Puggit	Italian Greyhound	x	Pug
Puggle	Beagle	x	Pug
Puginese	Pekingese	x	Pug
Pugland	Pug	x	W. Highland White Terrier
Pugottie	Pug	x	Scottish Terrier

CROSSBREEDS	PUREBRED PARENTS		
Pugshire	Pug	x	Yorkshire Terrier
Pugzu	Pug	x	Shih Tzu
Pushon	Bichon Frise	x	Pug
Raggle	American Rat Terrier	x	Beagle
Rashon	American Rat Terrier	x	Bichon Frise
Ratapap	American Rat Terrier	x	Papillon
Ratapin	American Rat Terrier	x	Min. Pinscher
Ratcha	American Rat Terrier	x	Chihuahua
Ratshi Terrier	American Rat Terrier	x	Shih Tzu
Ratshire Terrier	American Rat Terrier	x	Yorkshire Terrier
Rattle	American Rat Terrier	x	Poodle
Rattle Griffon	American Rat Terrier	x	Brussels Griffon
Rottaf	Afghan Hound	x	Rottweiler
Rotterman	Doberman Pinscher	x	Rottweiler
Rustralian Terrier	Australian Terrier	x	Jack Russell Terrier
Saint Berdoodle	Poodle	x	Saint Bernard
Saint Weiler	Rottweiler	x	Saint Bernard
Schapso	Lhasa Apso	x	Min. Schnauzer
Schipapom	Pomeranian	x	Schipperke
Schipese	Maltese	x	Schipperke
Schipperpoo	Poodle	x	Schipperke
Schnautzu	Min. Schnauzer	x	Shih Tzu
Schneagle	Beagle	x	Min. Schnauzer
Schnekingese	Min. Schnauzer	x	Pekingese
Schnese	Havanese	x	Min. Schnauzer
Schnocker	Cocker Spaniel	x	Min. Schnauzer
Schnoodle	Min. Schnauzer	x	Poodle
Schnu	Min. Schnauzer	x	Shiba Inu
Schweenie	Dachshund	x	Shih Tzu
Scoland Terrier	Scottish Terrier	x	W. Highland White Terrier
Scoodle	Poodle	x	Scottish Terrier
Scotchon	Bichon Frise	x	Scottish Terrier
Scotti Apso	Lhasa Apso	x	Scottish Terrier
Scottish Skye Terrier	Scottish Terrier	x	Skye Terrier
Sharbo	Boston Terrier	x	Chinese Sharpei
Sharmatian	Chinese Sharpei	x	Dalmatian
Sharp Eagle	Beagle	x	Chinese Sharpei
Shelaussie	Min. Australian Shepherd	x	Shetland Sheepdog
Shelchon	Bichon Frise	x	Shetland Sheepdog
Shelillon	Papillon	x	Shetland Sheepdog
Sheltidoodle	Poodle	x	Shetland Sheepdog
Shepadoodle	German Shepherd	x	Poodle
Sheprador	Australian Shepherd	x	Labrador Retriever
Shibos	Boston Terrier	x	Shiba Inu
Shichi	Chihuahua	x	Shih Tzu
Shiffon	Brussels Griffon	x	Shih Tzu
Shih Apso	Lhasa Apso	x	Shih Tzu
Shichon	Bichon Frise	x	Shih Tzu
Shihmo	American Eskimo	x	Shih Tzu

CROSSBREEDS	PUREBRED PARENTS			CROSSBREEDS	PUREBRED PARENTS		
Shihpoo	Poodle	x	Shih Tzu	Toxirn	Cairn Terrier	x	Chihuahua
Shinese	Pekingese	x	Shih Tzu	Toy Fox Pinscher	Min. Pinscher	x	Toy Fox Terrier
Shipom	Papillon	x	Shiba Inu	Toy Poxer	Pug	x	Toy Fox Terrier
Shiranian	Pomeranian	x	Shih Tzu	Toy Rat Doxie	American Rat Terrier	x	Dachshund
Shocker	Cocker Spaniel	x	Shiba Inu	Tzu Basset	Basset Hound	x	Shih Tzu
Shorgi	Pembroke Welsh Corgi	x	Shih Tzu	Ultimate Mastiff	Dogue de Bordeaux	x	Neapolitan Mastiff
Shorkie Tzu	Shih Tzu	x	Yorkshire Terrier	Wapoo	Chihuahua	x	Poodle
Shug	German Shepherd	x	Pug	Wauzer	Min. Schnauzer	x	W. Highland White Terrier
Sibercaan	Canaan Dog	x	Siberian Husky	Weechon	Bichon Frise	x	W. Highland White Terrier
Siberian Indian Dog	Canaan Dog	x	Native American Indian Dog	Weepoo	Poodle	x	W. Highland White Terrier
Silkchon	Bichon Frise	x	Silky Terrier	Weeranian	Pomeranian	x	W. Highland White Terrier
Silkese	Maltese	x	Silky Terrier	Weimardoodle	Poodle	x	Weimaraner
Silkin	Japanese Chin	x	Silky Terrier	Welchon	Bichon Frise	x	Welsh Terrier
Silkinese	Pekingese	x	Silky Terrier	Welshund	Dachshund	x	Welsh Terrier
Silkland Terrier	Silky Terrier	x	W. Highland White Terrier	Weshi	Shih Tzu	x	W. Highland White Terrier
Silky Cocker	Cocker Spaniel	x	Maltese	West of Argyll Terrier	Beagle	x	W. Highland White Terrier
Silky Jack	Jack Russell Terrier	x	Silky Terrier	Westie Laso	Lhasa Apso	x	W. Highland White Terrier
Silky Lhasa	Lhasa Apso	x	Silky Terrier	Whoodle	Poodle	x	Wheaten Terrier
Silky Tzu	Shih Tzu	x	Silky Terrier	Wire Fox Pinscher	Min. Pinscher	x	Wire Fox Terrier
Silkzer	Min. Schnauzer	x	Silky Terrier	Wirelsh Terrier	Welsh Terrier	x	Wire Fox Terrier
Skilky Terrier	Scottish Terrier	x	Silky Terrier	Woodle	Poodle	x	Welsh Terrier
Skipshzu	Schipperkee	x	Shih Tzu	Wowauzer	Min. Schnauzer	x	Welsh Terrier
Skypoo	Poodle	x	Skye Terrier	Yochon	Bichon Frise	x	Yorkshire Terrier
Sniffon	Brussels Griffon	x	Min. Schnauzer	Yoranian	Pomeranian	x	Yorkshire Terrier
Snorkie	Min. Schnauzer	x	Yorkshire Terrier	Yorchon	Bichon Frise	x	Yorkshire Terrier
Soft-Coated Golden	Golden Retriever	x	Wheaten Terrier	Yorkie Apso	Lhasa Apso	x	Yorkshire Terrier
Soft-Coated Wheatzer	Min. Schnauzer	x	Wheaten Terrier	Yorkie Russell	Jack Russell Terrier	x	Yorkshire Terrier
Spantriever	English Cocker Spaniel	x	Labrador Retriever	Yorkieton	Coton de Tulear	x	Yorkshire Terrier
Springerdoodle	English Springer Spaniel	x	Poodle	Yorkillon	Papillon	x	Yorkshire Terrier
Swheat-N-Poo	Poodle	x	Wheaten Terrier	Yorkinese	Pekingese	x	Yorkshire Terrier
Taco Terrier	Chihuahua	x	Toy Fox Terrier	Yorkipoo	Poodle	x	Yorkshire Terrier
Tibetoodle	Poodle	x	Tibetan Terrier	Yorktese	Maltese	x	Yorkshire Terrier
Torkie	Toy Fox Terrier	x	Yorkshire Terrier	Zuchon	Bichon Frise	x	Shih Tzu

Poogle

Sheprador

Yorkipoo

Health Matters

While crossbreeds may benefit from hybrid vigor, they're not immune from the hereditary headaches of their purebred parents. It's best to do your research: before adopting a dog, be sure that the parents have been screened for possible ailments—and that the dog is happy and healthy. Here are recommended health tests for each of our featured crossbreeds.

Australian Labradoodle As a precaution against hip and elbow dysplasia, along with eye disease, ensure that both parents have obtained clearances for these disorders before breeding.

Bagle Hound Basset Hounds and Beagles commonly share obesity, hip dysplasia, back problems, and slipping kneecaps (also known as luxating patellas). Choose from a litter with slender, active parents who are free from such discomforts.

Brat Since Boston Terriers often experience breathing problems, confirm that the Terrier parent has been scanned for brachycephalic syndrome, and check that the puppy's nostrils aren't pinched and that he or she can breathe easily. Additionally, be sure that both parent breeds have been examined for slipping kneecaps and mange.

Cavachon Both Bichon Frises and Cavaliers can suffer from congenital cataracts and slipping kneecaps, so look for parents that have been cleared of both disorders. Also, Cavaliers have a high incidence of a hereditary heart problem called mitral valve insufficiency, so it's advisable that the Cavalier parent undergo a heart test.

Cavapoo Given that knee problems commonly afflict both parents, it's best that they have knee checkups before breeding. Also, the Cavalier parent should be examined for heart problems, which are sometimes spotted in the breed and may be passed to a hybrid.

Chesador Both Chesapeake Bay Retrievers and Labrador Retrievers have a predisposition toward hip and elbow dysplasia, as well as eyelid problems. Be sure that the parents obtain clean bills of health for their hips, elbows, and eyes.

Chiweenie Pick a puppy with a shorter back, to avoid some of the spinal problems associated with long backs. Avoid one with a large soft spot in his or her head, or that has hydrocephalus, which is typically signaled by an enlarged head and eyes that are the opposite of crossed. Both parent breeds are prone to slipping kneecaps and dry eyes, so hip and eye exams for both are a must.

Cockalier Choose a litter from parents that have been tested for hereditary problems common to both Cockers and Cavaliers: hip dysplasia, slipping kneecaps, and eyelid problems. The Cavalier parent should also have a heart test, because Cavaliers have a hereditary heart problem that may or may not be transmitted to a hybrid.

Cockapoo Cocker Spaniels and Poodles share several eye problems, including hereditary blindness, as well as slipping kneecaps. Both parents should have eye- and knee-health screenings.

Comfort Retriever Because both parent breeds are susceptible to hip dysplasia, eye disorders, and skin problems, choose parents that have health clearances for hips and eyes, and that appear to have healthy skin and coats.

Doxiepoo Dachshunds and Poodles are prone to slipping kneecaps, dry eyes, and seizures; parents should be screened for these disorders. Doxiepoos with long spines can also suffer from back problems, so choose a puppy with a shorter back.

Frenchie Pug Because both parent breeds can suffer from hip dysplasia, slipping kneecaps, vertebra problems, and allergies, both parents should be screened for these disorders. Both parent breeds also are noted to suffer from brachycephalic syndrome, which may require corrective surgery to allow the dog to breathe normally. When selecting a puppy, avoid any that make loud wheezing or breathing noises, or that have pinched nostrils.

Goldendoodle Golden Retrievers and Poodles share a few health concerns, so look for dogs that have parents who are free of hip, elbow, and eye disease.

Jackabee Because both parent breeds have hereditary glaucoma and slipping kneecaps, they should both be screened for eye and knee disorders.

Jackapoo Jack Russells and Poodles have a few hereditary problems in common, slipping kneecaps in particular. Both parents should undergo knee tests.

Jack Chi Slipping kneecaps have been known to bother both Jack Russells and Chihuahuas, so a vet should vouch for the knee health of both parents.

Labbe Labradors and Beagles share several inherited problems, including hip dysplasia, blindness, eyelid problems, slipping kneecaps, and low thyroid. Both parents should obtain clean bills of health for their hips, eyes, knees, and thyroids.

Labmaraner Hip dysplasia and eyelid problems have troubled both Labradors and Weimaraners. To be safe, have both parents' hips and eyes checked.

Labradoodle As Labradoodles are susceptible to health problems shared by both parent breeds—namely a blinding disease called progressive retinal atrophy, knee problems in Medium and Miniature Labradoodles, and hip dysplasia in Standards—be sure that each parent is thoroughly screened.

Lhasapoo The Lhasa Apso and Poodle parents should be screened for slipping kneecaps and eye disorders, which have a history of afflicting both parents.

Malshi As both Maltese and Shih Tzus suffer from allergies and slipping kneecaps, it's best to check both parents prior to breeding.

Maltapoo Both parent breeds are prone to slipping kneecaps, as well as several eyelid problems and a hip ailment called Legg-Perthes disease. Look for a puppy from parents cleared of knee, hip, and eye problems.

Maltipom Ensure your puppy's health by checking parents for slipping kneecaps and progressive retinal atrophy.

Papipoo Papillons and Poodles share a few hereditary problems, most notably slipping kneecaps, as well as seizures, blindness, and back problems. Both parents should be screened for knee, eye, and back disorders.

Pekeapoo Look for a puppy with front legs that are not twisted, and that are as long as the hind legs. Also favor one with a longer muzzle. Both eyelid problems and slipping kneecaps can occur in both Pekes and Poos, so look for parents that have had their eyes and knees tested.

Poogle Poodles and Beagles share some hereditary problems, including hip dysplasia, slipping kneecaps, and eyelid disorders, so both parents should be looked over to rule out these problems.

Puggle Look for a puppy with a longer muzzle, wide open nostrils, and quiet breathing. Ideally, both parents should be screened for hip dysplasia as well.

Schnoodle Ideal parents will have been checked clear of a blinding disease called progressive retinal atrophy.

Silkchon Make an effort to screen both parents for slipping kneecaps and Legg-Perthes disease, which hinders the hip.

Tibetoodle Since slipping kneecaps, progressive retinal atrophy, and hip dysplasia are common to both parents, be sure to screen for all three.

Toy Fox Pinscher Both parents have a history of slipping kneecaps, hip dysplasia, and Legg-Perthes disease. Before selecting a puppy, the parents should have hip and knee checkups.

Whoodle Because Soft-Coated Wheaten Terriers and Standard Poodles both suffer from hip dysplasia and Addison's disease (an illness that affects the hormonal system), both parents should be declared free of these problems. Hereditary blindness has also been noted in both breeds, so parents should undergo eye examinations prior to breeding.

Yochon Slipping knees, hip dysplasia, and cataracts are illnesses commonly found in both Yorkshire Terriers and Bichon Frises, so confirm that the parents have been cleared by a vet for all three disorders before breeding.

Yorkipoo Yorkshire Terriers and Poodles share several hereditary problems, including slipping knees, eye problems, and a hip problem called Legg-Perthes disease. Both parents should be screened for each disorder.

Yorktese Due to the prevalence of slipping kneecaps, Legg-Perthes disease, and liver difficulties, choose a puppy whose parents have clean bills of health for their knees, hips, and livers.

Zuchon When choosing a litter, look for one with parents that have been tested for slipping knees, hip dysplasia, and cataracts, which are seen in both parents.

Labmaraner

Meet the Models

Special thanks to our team of stellar dog models, who fetched, snoozed, wrestled, high-fived, sprinted, chewed, played, swam, cuddled, jumped, drooled, wagged, frolicked, hung out, and were just plain great—all for the camera.

Mika
Cavachon p.25

Clementine
Papipoo p.29

Nikita
Chiweenie p.31

Jack
Lhasapoo p.35

Buddha
Lhasapoo p.35

Brenda
Lhasapoo p.35

Big Daddy
Lhasapoo p.35

Barron
Bagle Hound p.39

Dakota Betty
Comfort Retriever p.41

Dakota
Comfort Retriever p.41

Henri
Cockapoo p.45

Belly
Cockapoo p.45

Jasper
Labbe p.51

Tito
Yorkipoo p.53

Peanut
Australian Labradoodle p.57

Dash
Australian Labradoodle p.57

Peanut
Toy Fox Pinscher p.63

Fletcher
Goldendoodle p.65

Crema
Labmaraner p.69

Kobe
Tibetoodle p.73

Ed
Doxiepoo p.75

Billy
Poogle p.79

Robber
Frenchie Pug p.81

Marley
Cavapoo p.85

Daphne
Cavapoo p.85

Miles
Labradoodle p.89

Guramayle
Labradoodle Mini p.89

Kalib
Yochon p.95

Huck Finn
Jackabee p.97

Coco Sette
Zuchon p.101

Oreo
Malshi p.103

Gizmo
Maltipom p.107

Baxter
Jackapoo p.109

Saatchi
Pekeapoo p.113

Juno
Chesador p.115

Mileah
Cockalier p.119

Muffy
Maltapoo p.123

Chewy
Jack Chi p.127

Max
Schnoodle p.131

Lucca
Puggle p.133

Bula
Puggle p.133

Buster
Silkchon p.139

Rascal
Yorktese p.141

Grady
Whoodle p.145

Jax
Brat p.147

Coco
Chug p.151

Logos
Cockapoo p.151

Hanna
Chion p.151

Rocky
Doxiepoo p.151

Dusty
Goldendoodle p.152

Becky
Goldendoodle p.152

Mazie
Goldendoodle Mini p.152

Bella
Jack Chi p.152

Lola
Labradoodle p.153

Jimmy
Maltapoo p.153

Wyley
Oripei p.153

Harper
Poogle p.155

Mocha
Sheprador p.155

Chloe
Yorkipoo p.155

THE END

Index

Acknowledgments

Thanks to the following for their assistance, advice, or expertise: Aud & M, props; Corbis, additional photography (page 17, left and right; page 18, right; page 19, left and right; page 20, left and right; page 21, right); Ken DellaPenta, indexer; Fab Dog Inc., props; Garry Garner at the American Canine Hybrid Club, consultant; Getty Images, additional photography (page 18, left; page 21, left); Jax and Bones, props; Kanani Kauka, proofreader; Paco Collars, props; Danielle Parker, editorial support; Louise Thomas, photo researcher; Erin Zaunbrecher, proofreader.

Special thanks to Robbie Fullmer at Four Wet Feet for helping in the search for dog models.

Dog Companions

Dan and Nancy Ahern; Besty Ahlstrand; Stephen Barker; Becky Basque; Carissa Beecham and Matthew Lechowick; Yvette Bonaparte and Liam Thor; Boyd and Samantha Burggrabe; Jesse and Michelle Chavez; Gail and John Cleveland; Eric Darius; Kiley DeMond; Caryn and Paul Franson; Connie Freeman; Joseph Gamino; Mo Ghotbi; Sue Gonzalez; Diana Huett; Denise and Stephane Jourdaine; Jacquie Kim; Heather King; Jeanne and Tom Kucsak; Allison and Lorrie Landis; Carol and Don Laucella; Darielle Ledezma-Perez; Elena Matsis; Jessica and Jonathan McCormick; John and Peggy McGarrahan; Julie McKernan; Michelle Mertz and Chris Micallef; Cale and Lauren Miller; Camela Mong; Cynthia Morgan; Karen Murray and Jeff Benson; Michael Ortega and Stephanie Hughes; Marilyn Oshinko; Sharon Pancio, Colleen Riley, Misha Riley, and Simone Riley; Lisa Radler and Sara Watson; Lana Repert; AnMarie Rodgers and Jewlia Eisenberg; Davone Rodgers; Victor Romero; Andrea Saint Ives; Mark and Nancy Scoggin; Anne Scott; Shawna Scott; Claudia Sutton; Vanessa Thomas; Sharon Umayam; Dany Vallerand; Melanie Villenueva and Edvin Talusan; Karen Wolowicz; Wilfred, Gladys, and Kristy Young.

People Models

Besty Ahlstrand, Hannah Alston, Stephen Barker, Kiley DeMond, Joseph Gamino, Mo Ghotbi, Sue Gonzalez, Carla Johnson, Marisa Kwek, Allison Landis, Darianna Isabella Perez Ledezma, Ed Meng, Michael Orange, Michael Ortega, Lucie Parker, Misha Riley, Andrea Saint Ives, Liam Thor, John Torchio, Vivian Wong.